BY JEANETTE FARRELL

Invisible Enemies: Stories of Infectious Disease

Invisible Allies: Microbes That Shape Our Lives

The author enjoying a microbe-made meal with her family

INVISIBLE ALLIES

Microbes That Shape Our Lives

JEANETTE FARRELL

Farrar Straus Giroux • New York

For my mother, with love

Distributed in Canada by Douglas & McIntyre Publishing Group
Printed in the United States of America
Designed by Nancy Goldenberg
First edition, 2005
1   3   5   7   9   10   8   6   4   2

www.fsgkidsbooks.com

Library of Congress Cataloging-in-Publication Data
Farrell, Jeanette.
    Invisible allies : microbes that shape our lives / Jeanette Farrell.— 1st ed.
        p.   cm.
    ISBN-13: 978-0-374-33608-0
    ISBN-10: 0-374-33608-3
    1. Microbiology—Juvenile literature.   2. Microorganisms—Juvenile literature.
I. Title.

QR57.F37 2005
579—dc22

                                        2004053750

Acknowledgments

The kindness of many people made this work possible. To name and thank but a few: Julia and Susan Grace generously welcomed me to their farm, and Monica Page patiently shared with me her cheese-making expertise. Ed Wood fielded many questions and inspired me with his wonderful books and love of bread. Tore Midtvedt shared with me his fascination for germ-free animals. Jim Pitts amazed me with his boundless enthusiasm for and knowledge of a subject generally ignored in polite company.

I also want to thank Nancy Freitag, Ted White, Lexy Taylor and her colleagues at King County, and my sister Pat Farrell for their essential help. And, of course, I feel very grateful for the tireless and very creative work of the whole team behind the book at Farrar, Straus and Giroux, especially Wesley Adams, Lisa Greenwald, Elaine Chubb, Janet Renard, Daniel Myers, Nancy Seitz, and Nancy Goldenberg.

I could never adequately thank Anna and Phoebe for their good-humored, patient support. And my gratitude to David is far beyond words.

Contents

INVISIBLE ALLIES

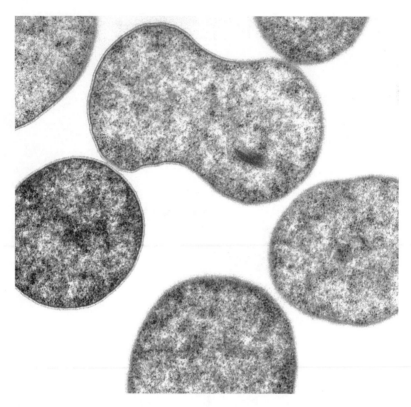

Pyrococcus furiosus: a microbe that not only lives but thrives at temperatures hot enough to boil water. Biologists used to think nothing could survive in such heat. But these bugs, which live on the ocean floor around deep-sea vents, have proven them wrong. Another surprising thing is that these microbes breathe sulfur instead of oxygen

Introduction

For creatures your size I offer
    a free choice of habitat,
so settle yourselves in the zone
    that suits you best, in the pools
of my pores or the tropical
    forests of arm-pit and crotch,
in the deserts of my fore-arms,
    or the cool woods of my scalp.
—W. H. AUDEN
    from "A New Year Greeting," 1969

More than one hundred trillion tiny creatures far too small for you to see live in and on you. Your body houses about ten times more microbes than you have cells. Some spots host more guests than others: the "desert" of your back may contain as few as four hundred microbes per postage-stamp-sized piece of skin, but the hospitable "tropical forests" of your armpit may house more than three times that number. Our entire planet teems with invisible life: microbes, or microorganisms, live in the absolute dark two thousand yards deep in the ocean, in hot springs that heat nearly to boiling, and in the icy interior of Antarctica. Microbes strive to live everywhere, and they make no exception for our bodies.

Before the thought of these creepy visitors sends you running, somewhat futilely, for a bar of soap, consider this: the successful persistence of microbes is responsible for life on Earth. Microbes release oxygen into the air we breathe, they rid the world of noxious mounds of dead plants and animals, and they free up the parts of those dead things so that we can use them to make our bodies. Those microbes living in our gut digest our foods, make vitamins we need, and hold other unwelcome microbial invaders at bay. It is very likely that if all other forms of life were to die, the microbes would go right on enjoying planet Earth in our absence. If the microbes were to die off, however, plants, animals, and humans would not stand a chance.

This book shines a spotlight on the essential work of our invisible companions to show how we humans depend on microbes every day, most intimately. While it is certainly true that some microbes have earned human enmity—some ferment our sweat until it stinks, raise pimples on our faces, rot holes in our teeth, sicken us and kill us—far more of their uncountable numbers live among us peacefully, nearly all of the time. One microbiologist in what he called the 1941 Census of Bacteria in the United States tried to calculate the total numbers of helpful and harmful bacteria. He concluded:

If we summarize all these data in two groups, good bacteria versus bad bacteria, we find more than 10,031,000 quintillion good ones against less than 308 quintillion bad ones. In other words, out of every 30,000 bacteria in the United States, 29,999 are harmless, useful or even necessary for our lives while one is a disease bacterium. That is not a bad record compared with that of the human race. In 1942, there were 7,569 persons convicted of murder in the United States, or 1 out of every 17,000. Considering that the proportion of harmful bacteria in our estimate is certainly too high, it would only be fair to admit that bacteria are certainly no more dangerous to humanity than man himself.

In the years since this census was conducted, we have learned more and more about our dependence on these unseen creatures. We have found that they live in our bodies at many times the density once expected. Not only do they digest our food but they actually help direct the development of our gut. Interactions with these microbes train our immune responses. Outside of the body, microbes decompose our sewage and our garbage. We are just beginning to explore how microbes' talents at recycling can help us clean up the toxic wastes of modern life.

Because they are about one hundred times too small to see with the naked eye, microbes often get little credit for their work. Humans had been brewing and baking with yeast and transforming milk into cheese for thousands of years before anyone realized these acts were the result of tiny, invisible forms of life.

The first human being to explore the world of the microbes, Antony van Leeuwenhoek, certainly did not set out to look for unseen living creatures. Leeuwenhoek sold cloth for a living in the Dutch town of Delft in the seventeenth century. He used small lenses to magnify fabric threads so that he could better evaluate the cloth's quality. Leeuwenhoek had never gone to college and certainly had never studied science, but his curiosity was his teacher. The world the lens opened to him was irresistible. Leeuwenhoek began to fashion lenses with more and more precision, and he trained them on objects wherever his curiosity took him. He even rigged up a microscope so that he could watch gunpowder explode! Among the many questions that occurred to him and that he tried to explore with his marvelous microscopes was, What gives foods flavor? Leeuwenhoek began to grind spices, suspend them in water, and examine their particles for clues.

Leeuwenhoek's homemade microscopes were merely brass rectangles no bigger than a postmark, with a spherical glass lens the size of a BB set in the middle. He mounted a screw parallel to the plate and stuck samples on its point. To make the apparatus, he forged and smithed the brass and the screw, as well as melted and shaped the glass for the lens. And he persisted until he was able to create a device that could accurately magnify images three hundred times! One day in the spring of 1676 Leeuwenhoek examined some pepper mixed with water that had been sitting around for about three weeks. Much to his surprise, when he peered through his lens into a thin glass tube of the wa-

Antony van Leeuwenhoek

ter (he made tubes as thin as a hair in a horse's tail), he found not merely the austere geometry of the lifeless spice, but a squirming, living world never before seen by human eyes.

> *I saw therein, with great wonder, incredibly many very little animalcules, of divers sorts . . . These animalcules are very odd in their motions, oft-times tumbling all around sideways . . . [One type was] incredibly small; nay, so small, in my sight, that I judged that even if 100 of these very wee animals lay stretched out one against another, they could not*

reach to the length of a grain of coarse sand; and if this be true, then ten hundred thousand of these living creatures could scarce equal the bulk of a coarse sand-grain.

Leeuwenhoek was seeing bacteria—the most numerous of all microbes, so small that more than fifty thousand could fit on the period at the end of this sentence—and he was the first human being to do so.

Not only did Leeuwenhoek see the microbe world, but he also described it, in precise detail, in letters he wrote to the great thinkers of his time. His descriptions were so careful and accurate that today's scientists can recognize all the distinct categories of microbes among them. Leeuwen-

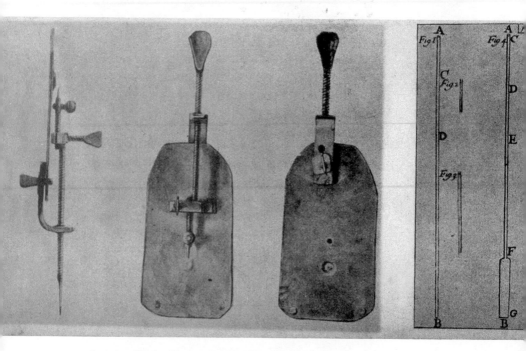

Leeuwenhoek microscope and glass tube for samples

hoek did wonderful sketches of the various shapes of bacteria: he drew the little spheres called cocci, the spirals known as spirochetes, and the long rectangular cells known as rods. He also described and drew protozoa—highly organized one-celled animals that are about ten to a hundred times bigger than bacteria—as well as algae—photosynthetic plantlike organisms that can be microscopic or visible to the naked eye. And he described the fungi, a group that includes molds, which sometimes grow so numerous on foods that no microscope is necessary to see them. Fungi can be as large as mushrooms or as small as single-celled yeast—just ten times as big as bacteria. (The one category of microbe Leeuwenhoek could not see was the virus, as viruses, which are merely bits of genetic information in a protein envelope, can be seen only by means of an electron microscope.)

Leeuwenhoek's discoveries elicited surprise, disbelief, and sometimes disgust. He sent his letters from his home in Delft to the Royal Society in London, a distinguished group of the best thinkers of the time. The members of the Royal Society wrote back their amazement and shock that in a simple drop of water there could be so many living creatures. It was very difficult to believe that their world contained living things they had never imagined that were so common, so many, and so small! To convince the thinkers, Leeuwenhoek first described his elaborate methods of estimating the size of the things that he viewed through his tiny lens. He explained that a drop of water was about the size of a pea; that a millet seed was about one-hundredth the size of a pea; and that he took a sample of water the size of a millet seed, divided it up among thirty of his glass tubes for viewing, and counted the number of creatures he could see in each tiny sample.

To further prove himself, the microscopist then called in prominent members of his community to bear witness that they, too, had seen the tiny creatures with their own eyes. (He even glued a bunch of millet seeds together to demonstrate their volume for his witnesses.) Leeuwenhoek's pastor wrote in his letter of witness, "I did see a very great number of little animals moving in that water, so many that I could not possibly number them, and to my sight they seemed to exceed the number expressed in his fore-mentioned letter." Then when Leeuwenhoek added vinegar to kill the creatures in order to prove that they were living things, the pastor was even more impressed: "I did see those little animals in the water, but they did not move at all (being killed by the vinegar) which I beheld with admiration, that in so small a quantity of water I should see such a vast number of those little animals."

Leeuwenhoek himself expressed such wonder in his letters that it was clear he could scarcely believe his eyes. He wrote:

For my own part, I can say with truth, that the smallest sort of which I shall here speak, I see alive and exhibit as plainly to my eyes as one sees, with the naked eye, little flies or gnats sporting in the air, though they may be more than a hundred million times less than a coarse grain of sand; for not only do I observe their progression, both when they hurry, and when they slow down, but I see them turn about, and stand still, and in the end even die; and those that are of a bigger sort, I can also see running along as plain as you see mice.

Leeuwenhoek's illustrations of bacteria

The creatures Leeuwenhoek saw populated not just rainwater but also nearly every substance he viewed, including (to name only some of the things he explored) river water, well water, sea water, and pond water; water mixed with ginger, with clove, and with nutmeg as well as with pepper; the feces of pigeons, chickens, frogs, cows, horses, and humans; and vinegar. And then he turned his lens to his own mouth. In one of the many descriptive letters he wrote telling the world of his discoveries, Leeuwenhoek wrote about what he found when he looked at the scum on his own teeth after he refrained from cleaning them for three days: "I then most always saw, with great wonder, that in the said matter there were many very little living animalcules, very prettily a-moving. The biggest sort . . . had a very strong and swift motion, and shot through the water (or spittle) like a pike does through the water . . . The second sort . . . oft-times spun round like a top . . . and these were far more in number." And in the scum on the teeth of an old man who never cleaned them, Leeuwenhoek saw "an unbelievably great company of living animalcules, a-swimming more nimbly than any I had ever seen up to this time . . . Animalcules were in such enormous numbers, that all the water . . . seemed to be alive."

If the thought of these creatures swarming about on your teeth makes you squeamish, you are not alone. Although it would be two hundred more years before Robert Koch and Louis Pasteur, through careful, clever experiments, discovered that some of these creatures caused specific diseases, Leeuwenhoek did try to dispel the microbes from his teeth

being paid in scientific
o the recovery and utiliza-
tile constituents of coal,
ost universally lost in the
d attention some months
ary of industrial progress,
Scotch iron masters had
ethods for the recovery of
te gases of their blast fur-
roportionate waste of val-
the coking of coal. The
in face of the existence of
voiding it, is quite out of
n spirit of the times, and
revolution of the careless
important the question of
will appear from the fol-
er on "A New Process for
ry of the Volatile Constitu-
by Mr. T. B. Lightfoot be-
Arts:
nting out the necessity that
d economical method for
ts now almost universally
, and showing that in the
e the money value of this
s. 6d. per ton of iron pro-
ibe the process recently in-
use by Mr. J. Jameson, of
ugh recovery ovens have
or some time, they had not
of favor in this country,
ense attending their adop-
entirely inapplicable; but
y a slight and inexpensive
it could therefore be at once
e present ovens, which are
ty of dealing with 20,000,-
If this were done, the value
btained, would, at existing
£3,250,000, while a large
as, which, taken at the ex-
er 1,000 cubic feet, would
ld also be made available.
tention to the applications
s, which, instead of black-
urface of the country and
at present, would give us
le illuminating and lubri-
are now greatly dependent
g supply of spring oil in
, which is much wanted for
s well as for many indus-
produced in large quanti-
estimated from the experi-
that if the ammonia from
t in this country was util-
uld add £50,000,000 worth
uce. With regard to the

THE GERM THEORY OF DISEASE.—Mr. P. Casa-
major lately gave an instructive discourse on this interesting theme before the Alumni Association of the
Long Island College Hospital, in which he sketched
the history of the theory and its recent development
at the hands of Messrs. Pasteur and Koch.

The lecturer noticed that belief in the doctrine that
some diseases were due to minute organisms was held
in the remote past, and could be traced to the century
before the time of Christ when Varro, a Roman nat-
uralist, expressed belief in pathogenic micro-organisms, describing how minute germs in the mud of
swamps, which dried and was blown about by the
wind, might be absorbed in the body and cause disease. The next record on the subject was made in
1675. Spallanzani seems to have found out that the
decomposition of meats and vegetables was due to
minute organisms, and that boiling infusions of them
retarded their growth, and the liquid, by being her-
metically sealed, could be kept for an indefinite
length of time. Latour discovered the yeast plant
in 1836, and the mode of propagation by budding.
Pasteur, however, carried the study of germs farther
than any one else. As a result of his experiments,
the silk industry was restored to the south of France,
where it had been nearly destroyed by a disease
among the silkworms and moths, caused by a species
of protozoa. He also discovered that a fungus yeast
plant caused alcoholic fermentation. He made a
wide and thorough study of bacteria, showing how
different temperatures develop different varieties.
Their increase was by fission. Each one divided into
two, and each of these again separated into two, so
that in twenty-four hours from a single bacterum
came 16,770,000, and from these in another twenty-
four hours 288,000,000,000 would be produced. Pasteur studied the germ theory of disease by experiments with sheep afflicted with the carbuncular disease, or malignant pustule. He found it was caused
by the *bacillius anthracis*, which was found in the
blood of the dead animals when examined with the
microscope. This as surely caused the carbuncular
disease as trichinae caused trichinosis. Chicken
cholera was caused by special organisms, as many
experiments showed. The lecturer spoke of the work
of Pasteur in finding out a method of inoculation for
the carbuncular disease in sheep, caused by the
bacillus anthracis. Pasteur shared with Darwin the
honor of being the greatest investigator of nature of
this century. His great discovery was the attenua-
tion of anthrax virus. In the following year 85,000
sheep were vaccinated with it, and by the end of
1882, 400,000 sheep had been successfully inoculated.
Pasteur received much detraction at the hands of
eminent scientific men, but his discoveries have not
been successfully disputed. Lately he has made
beautiful discoveries in regard to rabies and kindred
diseases, and especially in the so-called red diseases
among pigs.

In closing, the lecturer referred to the discovery
of Dr. Koch that tubercular consumption was due to
an exceedingly minute bacillus, which had a great
weight of proof in its favor.

---

all situations where the
suitable, as, for examp
stations, public halls,
etc. The fundamental
consists in the introdu
proper proportions to
the utilization of the p
purposes; first, to heat
and gas before their u
ond, to establish and n
of the apartment, for
combustion, after perfe
ing the entering air an
considerably reduced i
ing a current of air fro
It will thus appear th
gas burner not only o
apartment, but materi
ventilation.

The burner proper
supplying a series of t
ring at the orifices of v
an air chamber surro
tubes; a central regen
a suction chimney le
The action is substant
air entering their resp
the heating chamber, a
but in their ascent to
highly heated, their te
the waste products in
about 1,600° Fah. Th
der of porcelain, and
this, descends into the
the regenerative heatir
chimney by way of a
The burner is jacketed
manner as to leave an
of cooler air to ascend
the burner, and also to
supply to the flame. T
rests a cylinder of gl
from the action of th
white and extremely s
bly diffused.

The results obtained
generative principle (th
ing air and gas by th
combustion products)
and may be summed
mination ; economy i
steadiness of flame; o
ization of combustion

At the present time
Light Co., of Philade
sizes of these burners.

	Consum
No. I	.50 c
No. IIA	.35
No. II	.25
No. III	.14

The light yielded by
fore be seen to be at th
foot. The ordinary g
per cubic foot of gas
normal gas being from

Mention in the May 1884 edition of the journal *Manufacturer and Builder* of a new scientific theory: "The Germ Theory of Disease"

with vigorous vinegar washes and gulps of hot coffee. As fascinating as he found their world, he did not want them living in his mouth.

Since the seventeenth century, scientists have gone on to prove that some microbes cause disease, spoil food, and in

LEEUWENHOEK'S CURIOSITY

Until the last hours of his ninety years of life, Leeuwenhoek was still actively telling the world about microbes. He not only dictated two more letters about his observations from his deathbed but also bequeathed to the Royal Society a collection of twenty-six microscopes and some samples he had made. In all, in his lifetime, historians estimate Leeuwenhoek made about five hundred microscopes. Many were left to his daughter, and when she died they were auctioned off along with some of the samples that Leeuwenhoek left on their little screws. The diversity of the samples he left behind gives us a sense of the breadth of his interests.

Just in the collection given to the Royal Society, the samples are as follows:

- Globules of Blood, from which its Redness proceeds.
- A thin Slice of Wood of the Lime-Tree, where the Vessels conveying the Sap are cut transversely.
- The eye of a Gnat.
- A crooked Hair, to which adheres a Ring-Worm, with a piece of the Cuticle.
- A small Hair from the Hand, by which it appears those Hairs are not round.

fact rot the teeth they live on—but they have also found that all other forms of life depend on the microbes. We now have better reasons for Leeuwenhoek's ambivalence: we know that our dependence on microbes is an uneasy one. We need the microbes in our gut to help us digest our food,

---

- Flesh of the Codfish (*Cabeljaeuw*) shewing how the Fibres lie oblique to the Membranes.
- An Embrio of Cochineal, taken from the Egg, in which the Limbs and Horns are conspicuous.
- Small Pipes, which compose the Elephant's tooth.
- Part of the Crystalline Humour, from the Eye of a Whale.
- A Thread of Sheeps-Wool, which is broken, and appears to consist of many lesser Threads.
- The Instrument, whence a Spider spins the Threads, that compose his Web.
- A Granade, or Spark made in Striking Fire.
- The Vessels in a leaf of Tea.
- The *Animalcula in Semine Masculino*, of a Lamb taken from the Testicle, *Jul.* 24. 1702.
- A Piece of the Tongue of a Hog, full of sharp Points.
- A Fibre of Codfish, consisting of long slender Particles.
- A Filament, conveying Nourishment to the Nutmeg, cut transversely.
- A Bunch of Hair from the Insect call'd a Hair-Worm.
- The Organ of Sight of a Flie.

but if too many slip into our bloodstream they could kill us. We use microbes to make our cheese, but the wrong one at the wrong time can turn it into poison. Microbes will eat our sewage, but they will also eat our water pipes.

The last ten years of the twentieth century saw an explosion of products created to generate profits from our microbial aversion. In the United States alone, about seven hundred new anti-microbial products have been introduced. We can buy everything from antibacterial soap and toothpaste to socks and steering wheels coated with poisons to kill whatever microbes happen along. From looking at our grocery store shelves, one would imagine we have entered into an all-out war. A few years ago, fear of microbial ambitions inspired a wealthy Californian couple to build their dream home coated with a substance to halt the growth of microbes. The cooking pans and mattress pads, the sinks, the carpets, the shelves in the wine cellar, the handrails and heating vents—all were designed to stop microbes in their tracks.

Those who study microbes look askance at these efforts as a waste of money and possibly dangerous. Removing the microbes that commonly live around us, very likely a community humans have come to tolerate, only clears the way for other, possibly less friendly members of their kind. Not only that, microbes learn to avoid microbe-killing substances, just as they have learned to avoid antibiotics. And microbes can pass around the methods they have learned. The result can be that when we really need to kill microbes to protect the very sick, our tools will no longer work. Students of the microbial world, who, like Leeuwenhoek, look beyond the limits of human vision, suggest that antimicrobial efforts can go too far; we must begin to appreciate that the vast majority of microbes are doing good things for us.

In this book we will examine not only the things that microbes do for us daily but also the changing ways in which we humans have thought about the microbes in our lives. We will take the example of lunch. As Leeuwenhoek discovered a whole invisible universe by turning his microscope on an unremarkable cup of water, in the pages to follow we will look at a lunch of a cheese sandwich and a chocolate bar, and see how microbes create it, digest it, decompose it, and make it available to become a new and usable part of the world again. By examining this simple meal, we can come to understand the depth of our dependence on these tiny creatures. Perhaps, like the members of the Royal Society, you will open your eyes to the microscopic world around us.

Penicillium roqueforti

Microbes at the Table

Cheese—milk's leap toward immortality.
—CLIFTON FADIMAN

The fact that we are desperately outnumbered by microbes means that one of the primary challenges for humans is to get to the food before the microbes do. There is no food we eat that a microbe does not desire. In fact, there is little on the earth a microbe would not eat. Thank goodness, though, for the microbes' wide-ranging appetites: their voraciousness means that most things are not permanent. Think of the pile of dead bodies, and dead plants, and leftover food, and boxes, and old notebooks, and you name it, that would cover the earth if microbes were not doing their hungry work!

Microbes would also eat living things, if they could, so living things protect their own cells against microbes. But once we kill our intended meal, be it a fish slashed with a knife or an apple plucked from a branch, our now-dead food is no longer protected from the microbe devourers. Its time is numbered in days or even in hours. And once the microbes start to eat, and increase in numbers, our meal is poisoned for us. The bottom line is this: humans must either eat it fast or make it last.

This effort to make food last has inspired diverse, complex, and surprising means of food preservation. One of the most astonishing is cheese.

Mother's milk is a complete food for young mammals. It is also a great food for microbes. Most of us have had the experience of tipping a carton of cow's milk toward our cereal only to pour out a lumpy, sour-smelling mess instead of the sweet, smooth, white liquid we desired: the microbes have gotten to our milk before us. Although milk inside the udders of a healthy cow is sterile, once it leaves the cow's body, microbes, so persistent and ever present, swiftly find the rich fluid. They love to eat the milk's sugar, and they turn it into acid as they do, which separates the milk into thick white curds and clear runny whey. Pasteurizing milk—that is, heating it to 145 degrees Fahrenheit for thirty minutes and then cooling it—will kill most of the microbes that get into the milk in the process of milking, or any in the milk of a sick cow, and allow the milk to stay fresh a few days longer. Once pasteurized, milk can last a month unopened, or a week after you open the carton, but only if you store it at a nice cool temperature that discourages most microbes from growing. If the milk is transformed into cheese, however, that is a whole different matter. Much of the magic and mystery of cheese making can be summed up in this strange-sounding regulation: in the United States, if cheese is made from unpasteurized milk (that is, milk straight from the cow with all contaminating microbes still alive), it must be aged at least sixty days—no fewer—at a temperature of at least 35 degrees Fahrenheit—no cooler—before it can be considered safe to be sold. Keeping something as rich as milk for sixty days seems like a great way to make it good and rotten. And in fact, that is just the idea. The trick of cheese making is to encourage the right kind of microbes to grow and grow and grow—at their zenith, they number in the billions in a cheese—and in doing so, to prevent the growth of poisonous ones. If you are skilled and somewhat lucky, the result will be a bit of healthful, gourmet rot worth as much as a dollar an ounce.

Stopping by a fancy cheese counter and taking a deep breath will quickly let you in on what cheese makers are up to. For some types of cheese, the smellier, the more desirable. In a list of smells to detect in a cheese, one cheese book includes "mold-like," "musty," and "barnyardy." This makes it less surprising that the French word for one type of goat cheese translates as "horse dropping." Some cheeses are made from infecting the milk with the very microbes that make sweaty feet stink. But these strong and powerful smells come with unmatched flavors, leading cheese lovers to happily open their wallets and pay.

The gourmet may value the cheese maker's ability to create smells and tastes not found in anything else (that is edible), but humans began making cheese to turn milk into a food that lasts. It is suspected that humans figured out how to make cheeses as many as eight thousand years ago. Milk taken from animals, full of fat and protein, would have been a great source of nutrition but would have stayed fresh for a very short time in the days before refrigeration and pasteurization. In hot weather, milk could begin to sour within two or three hours. Animals gave milk for only part of the year, after they had their young in the spring. So milk was a seasonal food that could be enjoyed only when one had an animal close at hand. But at some point people realized the curds that formed after milk began to separate could be a good food in themselves. The acid made by the curdling bacteria kept most other microbes from growing, so the curds were a protein- and fat-rich food that was slow to rot. This type of bland, fresh cheese could last a week or two, longer in cool climates, less time in hot ones.

To make longer-lasting cheeses required discovering how to make firmer, longer-lasting curd that could then be infected by other healthful microbes as it aged. The secret was discovered in the fourth stomach of a calf. Rennet is a chemical produced by the calf's stomach lining to curdle its mother's milk and so change it from a liquid to a solid. This slows the milk's passage through the calf's digestive system, giving the calf's body more time to get all the nutrients from the milk. How did humans ever know what was going on in the fourth stomach of calves? Historians cannot know for sure, but they speculate that rennet was

Roman pottery cheese mold with holes for drainage

discovered by people who used animal stomachs to carry things in. Before the invention of pottery (and long before glass or plastic) a stomach, with the bottom tied off, made a strong bag for carrying drinks. But milk carried in a stomach bag eventually turned into curds and whey. One could imagine the annoyed surprise when some thirsty fellow opened his stomach bag to find his milk a solid lump floating in watery liquid. But then, when he tasted the white stuff, he would have found it nourishing and delicious. Over time people have discovered plant substances that also curdle milk: vegetable rennets can be made from thistles, nettles, figs, and safflowers. Chemicals produced by some fungi are also widely used as rennet. These other sources have been useful for cheese makers who did not want, or could not afford, to kill a young animal for rennet. Fungal rennet in particular is very cheap and has become popular with large manufacturers, but animal rennet is considered superior for making most cheese.

Although no one knows exactly when cheese making began in earnest, seven-thousand-year-old murals have been found showing people making cheese in caves in the northeastern Sahara Desert. Small pots of ancient cheese were

Cheese making circa 1548, from a German manuscript

found in the tomb of an Egyptian pharaoh from nearly five thousand years ago. Cheese quickly caught on in the Middle East and Europe as a great way to make milk last and a wonderful way to get protein without killing a valuable animal.

The ancient Romans developed the practice of cheese making and, in return, cheese nourished their empire. Romans learned how to cook the curds to improve their texture. They explored ways to vary cheese, all of which, unbeknownst to them, changed which microbes could live in the cheese. Encouraging the growth of some bacteria makes the curds too acid for others to grow. Salting a cheese prevents microbes that don't like salt. And aging a cheese will make it drier, eliminating microbes that need moisture. (Hard, dry Parmesan is aged for about two years, whereas soft Brie is aged for approximately one month.) After about three months of aging, all cheese is too dry and acid for any known bacteria to grow. But after they die the bacteria's disintegrating cells add flavor to the cheese.

Cheese proved a great food for the traveling Roman army. A piece of hard cheese in the knapsack was a sturdy and dense nutritious food that did not require cooking, was always ready to eat, and could last for months. And on their travels the Roman soldiers learned of other types of cheese made throughout Europe. One of the cheeses they loved was Roquefort.

Roquefort is a strong-flavored blue-veined cheese made in south-central France near the town of the same name. Fans of this cheese are so avid that Roquefort has been called the king of cheese. The Romans sang its praises when they conquered the area around Roquefort in the first century A.D., inspiring gourmets in Italy to try to import the cheese across many mountainous miles. One famous tale tells how the emperor Charlemagne stopped at a bishop's residence for a meal twelve hundred years ago. The bishop fed him some Roquefort, whereupon Charlemagne was so taken by the cheese he ordered the bishop to send him two cartloads of it every year. And today Roquefort fans in the United States do as the Romans and Charlemagne did, and import Roquefort cheese from France at the rate of about 440 tons each year.

The caves of Mount Combalou in southern France where Roquefort is made certainly are a fantastic place. It is easy to believe they can produce a cheese like no other. The original caves have been expanded to create a honeycomb of caverns, in some places eleven floors deep, all for the sake of producing Roquefort cheese. The caves open in a cliff and lead back to deep cracks in the earth that reach all the way up to the plains above. The wind is drawn through these fissures, causing a constant current of air to blow through the caves. These drafts, known in French as *fleurines*, are said to be key to creating the right environment for aging the cheese. When the natural caves became too crowded, the cheese makers dug their larger network but took care that all the caves were still fed by the *fleurines*. The conditions in the caves are the same year-round, a cool 48 degrees Fahrenheit, with a damp 96 percent humidity, making a retreat from summer heat and a shelter in winter. The caves are also a lovely place for the mold *Penicillium roqueforti* to grow.

Legend has it that the coolness of the caves led a shepherd to hide his lunch of curds and bread there one summer day, about two thousand years ago, and when he found his forgotten lunch, days later, the curds had turned a shocking shade of greenish-blue! (You yourself may have seen this type of mold not only in so-called blue cheese but also on old bread and forgotten oranges.) But the legendary shepherd, being hungry and perhaps somewhat daring, tasted his blue cheese anyway and found, to his surprise, that it was delicious! It was this accident, they say, that introduced the world to the king of cheese.

This legend has certainly captured people's imagination—some have gone so far as to say that the date the lunch was discovered was June 4 in the year 1070. Before you start planning your Roquefort Day party, however, note that this is about one thousand years after the Romans wrote of enjoying this cheese. Nevertheless, perhaps it was something like this shepherd's accident that led to the discovery of Roquefort.

The Roquefort cheese Charlemagne ate would have been made from the milk of the sheep that thrive in that region, milk that was curdled with rennet from lamb stomachs. Then the whey would have been drained from the curds, and the curds placed in something like a colander that would allow the whey to continue to drain out and also shape the cheese into a solid mass. After a few days, when the cheese was firm, and had been salted, it would have been moved to the cave, where the *fleurines* were called on to do their magic. Within hours of the cheese's arrival in the cave, the *Penicillium roqueforti* spores—very small, long-lasting seeds—borne aloft on the *fleurines*, would have settled on the cheese and begun to grow.

A fungus is the perfect microbe to take flight on a draft of air and settle down and grow in a cave. Perhaps you have done this experiment yourself: set aside two pieces of bread, one in the light, and one in the dark, and keep track of how quickly and thoroughly they mold. Hands down, the piece in the dark will become multicolored and furry with fungi much more quickly and more thoroughly than the piece in the light. Like many molds, *Penicillium roqueforti* likes it dark. This mold also prefers a cool, moist environment like that of Combalou. Mold spores are very light, so they are able to take off with the slightest breeze, and they are wrapped in a very tough coat that protects their important genetic material from drying out. They can stay aloft for forty-eight hours and last for years.

When an air-blown spore drops onto a thick disk of fresh sheep's cheese, it knows that it has found a good place to grow, and grow it does. First sprout the hyphae, or the white branching strands of the body of the mold that will spread through the cheese, taking in nutrients. When the mold is ready to reproduce, small treelike structures known as "fruiting bodies" grow off the hyphae. These will produce the spores. The fruiting bodies of molds in the genus *Penicillium* have long slender stalks that sprout many long thin branches at their tips. They look very much like tiny

Roquefort cheese ripening in the caves of Mount Combalou

brushes, hence their name: *penicillus* means "paintbrush" in Latin. The oval blue-green spores from which blue cheese gets its name form at the tip of each branch of the fruiting bodies. Each spore is only about four microns across, a hundred times too small to see with the naked eye, yet by the millions they form the rivers of blue in Roquefort. One body of mold alone can produce thousands of spores, all ready to blow away on the *fleurines* and turn yet another cheese blue.

The reason the name of this mold is so much like that of the drug penicillin is that it was the errant spore from one of *Penicillium roqueforti*'s cousins that led to the discovery of the antibiotic penicillin in 1928. The spore drifted into a dish in which a British bacteriologist, Alexander Fleming, was growing some disease-causing microbes. When Fleming looked at the plate, he found that a mold had begun to grow. (As you can imagine, it can be hard to keep wide-ranging mold spores away from food you put out for other microbes.) But rather than throwing the plate away because it had been contaminated, Fleming stopped to look and noticed that in the area around the mold the disease-causing microbe was unable to grow! This mold, he thought, seems to produce a substance that can kill germs. Fleming realized this might be a great way to kill microbes that were in humans. Within a few years this mold was being used as life-saving penicillin.

Originally Roquefort cheese was made just by leaving cheeses in the cave and relying on the *fleurines*. Over time, as making this cheese became more and more of a commercial enterprise, the cheese makers wanted to ensure that the mold made its way thoroughly through each and every cheese. So they began baking huge loaves of rye bread, ten to twenty pounds each, and leaving them in the cave to mold. Weeks later, they broke open the bread and mixed the mold into their cheese before bringing it to the cave to age for at least three months. And that is how the cheese is made to this day.

For most of the two thousand years during which Roquefort cheese has been made, no one even knew that microbes existed, much less what ones were responsible for creating the flavor of a particular cheese. As a result, cheese making was a process of trial and error, of remembering what had worked to make a good cheese once before and trying to repeat those same conditions. In the case of Roquefort, that meant making the cheese in those same caves, over and over again. Limburger, a German cheese populated by the stinky-feet microbe, was made by a "smear" technique: cheese makers would wash a good, stinky cheese in salt water and then rub that water over a fresh cheese. Other cheeses were covered with ash or wrapped in leaves. Still others were smoked, rubbed with salt, or dipped in brine. Some were aged for weeks, and others for months.

It was not until 1906, after at least nineteen hundred years of making Roquefort cheese, that an American scientist named Charles Thom identified and named the mold responsible for the cheese: *Penicillium* for the family of molds to which it was related, and *roqueforti* for the cheese. Thom was working for the U.S. Department of Agriculture on a project to explore the possibility of making Roquefort cheese in the United States. He described the need for the aging cheese to be kept cool and moist, as it was in the caves, and the fact that it was much better made with sheep's milk than with cow's. All of these secrets were well known to the cheese makers of Roquefort.

How the variables in cheese making affect the microbes involved is often mysterious, but the results can be profound. In a blue cheese like Roquefort, although the mold is the star player, it is far from the only microbe involved. A true Roquefort must be made from unpasteurized milk with whatever microbes are in it still alive and growing, and the proteins in the milk unchanged by heating. Most modern cheese makers also add a "starter" culture of microbes to control the process of "souring" the milk. By the

A.O.C.

You might think that now that we know in microscopic detail the secrets of the caves of Combalou, you could merely get a culture of *Penicillium roqueforti*—ordered on the Internet—and make yourself some Roquefort cheese at home. But making Roquefort is not so simple. Roquefort was the first of about forty French cheeses to have been given the designation *Appellation d'origine contrôlée*, or A.O.C. for short. These cheeses are of such consistent high quality that standards have been set for them to meet. Only by meeting these standards can the cheese receive the A.O.C. designation and be sold as "real" Roquefort in France.

The rules define both how the cheese is made and what qualities it must have. What milk is used to make the cheese is carefully specified, including what type of animals it comes from,

time the curds have drained and shaped, and the cheese has been salted and set aside to age, the lactic acid bacilli—the single-celled, stick-like creatures that curdle the milk with their acid—will probably number about three hundred million per thimbleful of cheese. They busily begin to re-model the structure of the curd by eating some of its pro-tein. Even after the cheese becomes too dry and acidic for the bacteria to survive, their dead bodies will continue to flavor the cheese: when these billions of cells burst upon death, they will release chemicals that will further break down the milk, adding flavor and smoothing the texture.

The bacteria will also help other microbes grow: some

---

what breed they are, and where they are raised. (Theoretically, any type of mammals' milk could be used, but because some animals are harder to milk than others, most cheese is made from cow, sheep, or goat milk. One researcher studying mammals' milk made a usable milking machine for guinea pigs, but it would take a few too many guinea pigs to make the twelve pounds of milk necessary for a two-pound Roquefort cheese.) Roquefort must be made from the milk of Lacaune sheep, raised in south-central France. It must be produced in Roquefort, from raw milk cultured by mold harvested from the caves of Combalou. The milk must be placed in the caves no more than eight days after being made and aged there for at least three and no more than nine months.

bacteria and yeasts will form carbon dioxide pockets in the cheese, opening up space for the blue molds to grow further and deeper. The lack of oxygen in these tight nooks and crannies prevents the growth of many common molds that might contaminate the cheese, but it allows *Penicillium roqueforti* to thrive. Salt-tolerant bacteria settle on the surfaces of cheeses that have been salted before they are stored, adding their products to the flavor mix. And all the while the *Penicillium roqueforti* is eating fats and proteins and leaving strong flavorful chemicals and blue spores in its wake.

The full extent of these interactions is not quite understood. As an expert on cheese microbiology once said, looking for the activity of a particular microbe in a cheese is a bit like looking for the Loch Ness monster. On the scale of a microbe, the cheese is as big as the 600-foot-deep lake in Scotland—it offers many living creatures plenty of room to hide. Tools for microbial explorations invented in the last twenty years of the twentieth century improved our ability to find and distinguish microbes, and some of these tools are being used to explore the microbial wilderness that is cheese. But understanding the complex interactions of microbes remains daunting. They work together in a remarkable cooperation we can observe only in glimpses.

One modern cheese maker, determined to better understand what was happening in her cheese, actually went out and earned herself a Ph.D. in microbiology. Mother Noella Marcellino, a Benedictine nun, had been making cheese in her abbey in Connecticut for twenty years when she began her studies. She had been through many heartaches and epiphanies as she struggled to make good cheese. At first, much of what she made had been suitable only for feeding the abbey's pigs. Then finally, with the help of a visiting Frenchwoman who taught her traditional cheese-making practices, Mother Noella began to make truly delicious cheese. Her star cheese is a quite complex one known as Saint-Nectaire.

Mother Noella Marcellino, with a wheel of her famous cheese

Saint-Nectaire is what is called a surface-ripened cheese. Rather than mixing microbes into the curds, as in Roquefort, makers of this type of cheese place microbes on, or attract them to, the surface of the cheese. The microbes then do their work from the outside in. Brie and Camembert are surface-ripened cheeses, for instance.

To make Saint-Nectaire, Mother Noella took raw cow's milk, added rennet (but no starter culture), and then relied on the bacteria present in the milk and the visitation of local molds and yeasts. No fewer than fourteen different

WHAT IS PROCESSED CHEESE?

Eaters who do not like surprises might prefer what is known as processed cheese. Processed cheese is made of unaged cheeses ground up with some aged cheese and mixed with chemicals to give it a smooth texture. It is pasteurized to kill the microbes and laced with salt and preservatives to keep it from rotting. The result is a bland, salty stuff that has something like the texture of cheese but none of the real flavor, and certainly no surprises. Processed cheese is simple to make on a mass scale, so it can be very profitable for food companies, and you will find a great deal of it on the shelves of your grocery store. Do not expect it to be anything like real cheese.

Real cheese requires careful attention to detail—the coddling of cows, the careful minding of pastures, and the patient coaxing of microbes. The best cheeses are created by small cheese makers who are in love with cheese and not afraid of very hard work.

molds and yeasts have been associated with the ripening of this cheese. It takes a remarkable faith in the natural world to set aside a disk of curdled milk in a warm room and expect it to become a Saint-Nectaire.

I can only imagine the excitement Mother Noella experienced when she began to explore her cheese with a light microscope and a scanning-electron microscope. These tools open a window into the microbe world, showing clearly where on the cheese each microbe is; how the various microbes are interrelating; and, if the cheese is examined day after day, when one microbe leaves and another moves in. After those years of courting the microbes, desperate for their invisible aid in making her cheese work, Mother Noella found that she could expose their mysterious ways.

Mother Noella's exploration revealed an amazing complexity of interactions in the rind of the cheese: each microbe prepared the way for the next. The yeasts were the first to appear; by the second day of aging, their oval shapes made the surface of the cheese look as if it were covered with balloons. Meanwhile, bacteria were beginning to grow inside the cheese, producing acid as they did. By day six, the cheese had grown a hairy white surface, a layer of mold known as *Mucor*. As this mold spread its long white tendrils, known as hyphae, out into the cheese, it "tilled" the surface, as Mother Noella describes it, digging into the cheese as a farmer plows a field and creating more places for yeast to grow. Another mold joined it, tucked under the *Mucor* hyphae. Then around day 31 there arose a third mold, somehow summoned by the work of the microbes that came before: *Trichothecium roseum*, which appeared as a faint wash of pink.

But these discoveries were only the beginning of her explorations. Mother Noella was curious about the differences between the microbes living on her cheese and those found on Saint-Nectaire in France, the birthplace of the cheese. Was there a difference between the native French mold and the native Connecticut mold? The nun flew to France and spent a year traveling from farm to farm, begging for permission to study the cheeses that the farmers made. The diversity she found was so astounding that she decided to narrow her scope by looking at just one microbe, *Geotrichum candidum*, an organism that has been classified sometimes as a yeast and sometimes as a mold but currently is considered a yeast. Whatever it is, this microbe is thought to contribute to every smear and mold-ripened cheese made, including Saint-Nectaire. Estimates of the number of different types of cheese made in France have ranged from 265 to 750. Charles de Gaulle, President of France from 1958 to 1969, is said to have claimed that a country that made so many cheeses could not be governed. Perhaps, but it is more certain that the number of different French cheeses cannot be counted. Even accounts of de Gaulle's famous quote vary—some say he claimed that France had 265 cheeses, another says 325, and still another 324. Mother Noella's research suggests that we should all give up counting. Among just seven dairies in one small region of France, Mother Noella found fourteen different varieties of *Geotrichum candidum*, each with different habits and quirks, and each therefore capable of creating a somewhat different cheese.

Have you ever had the experience of smelling something and immediately being taken back to a place in your past? The smell of pines, and you are at a vacation cottage? The scent of nutmeg, and it is Christmas Day? Cheese can powerfully evoke that sort of experience. The vast diversity of microbes, some encouraged to grow by one cheese maker's technique, others chased off by their neighbors, could each register as a distinct taste in that particular cheese maker's product and certainly might explain why a cheese from a particular farm has a taste like no other.

One New York writer recalls watching a French friend become teary with nostalgia when served a cheese from his hometown. I have had the experience, standing at a cheese counter in Seattle, of tasting a bit of goat cheese and finding myself whisked back to the Loire Valley in France, where I had visited goat cheese farms six years before. I have eaten a lot of goat cheese in the interim, but it was that particular Loire Valley goat cheese created by a very particular set of microbes that tweaked my flavor memory in a way that had the particular power to conjure up the whole experience for me.

The possibility of unique flavors should encourage new cheese makers who have just turned to the craft in parts of the world—like the United States—without France's renowned two-thousand-year-old cheese-making tradition. One of many such dairies is Moonstruck Farm, located on a lush and rugged island off the coast of British Columbia, Canada, not far from where I live.

When I arrived at tiny Moonstruck Farm on a wet day in spring, a calf had just been born. Unsteady, her honey-colored coat still dark from her first bath, she stood with the other calves exiled to their own company. When you are the calf of a dairy cow, your mom's milk is not for you. The milk of all the cows on Moonstruck Farm was destined to be made into Moonstruck cheese. To make up for this cruel reality of their business, owners Julia and Susan Grace have placed the calf pen adjacent to the cow pasture so that mothers can visit their offspring over the fence. "It makes them less anxious," says Julia. In addition to feeling more humane, that kindness may lead to better cheese. Perhaps less anxious cows give better milk.

One Vermont sheep farmer ships notes with her cheeses giving cheese sellers a little diary of the day on which the sheep produced the milk that created a particular cheese. The diaries contain what might matter to a sheep, the pasture where she ate, the season, and the weather. Even these simple things might affect the flavor of a cheese. As a result, each batch of cheese is a little different. It is a unique surprise!

The Graces' cheese-making day began with Julia and Susan watching over a cow in labor in the wee hours of the morning, then pulling her calf out after they had finished the morning feeding and milking. That day, in addition to cheese making, there would be more milking to do and many other chores: doctoring sick cows; making up cheese gift boxes to sell; managing their Web site; and cutting, wrapping, and pricing cheese wedges for the market. After all that, they had to unload a one-ton delivery of alfalfa bales, before sitting down for dinner, exhausted after another sixteen-hour workday. This is truly nonstop work. But, among the more than a thousand types of cheese made in the world, it is the cheese prepared by small cheese makers from the milk of small herds that captures the most

Cheese draining in the dairy at Moonstruck Farm as a member of the Jersey herd grazes outside

unique and valuable flavors produced courtesy of the microbe world.

The Moonstruck cheese-making room is situated with a view out over the Jersey cattle grazing in their pastures. On the day I visited, the Graces' cheese-making assistant, Monica Page, made all varieties of blue cheese from little soft cheeses known as Baby Blues to large disks of semisoft cheese named after a favorite cow called Blossom. Every-

All manner of blue cheese aging in the modern version of a cave: a large walk-in cooler

where around was the evidence of all the things that influence this cheese: the neat dairy was full of the rich, clean scent of milk. The lush grass of the pastures was alternately bathed in rain and blasted with sun on that blustery spring day. The cows, whom Julia and Susan try not to treat with antibiotics lest the drugs get into the milk and kill cheese-making microbes, roamed in and out of range of the calves. The calves investigated their new world with charming clumsiness, reminding us that their new lives, after all, were the inspiration for all this milk. It was not hard to imagine that on this temperate island, thick with cedar forests and moist with the salt air, some unique and benevolent microbe could visit the milk of these contented Jersey cows and bring to our tables a delicious, nutritious rot worthy of kings.

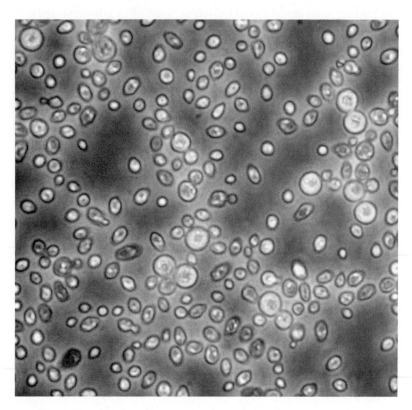

Saccharomyces cerevisiae, the type of yeast most commonly used to make bread

Our Daily Bread

*There's something alive in my kitchen
and it is 10,000 years old!*
—ED WOOD

On a ranch high in the mountains of Idaho is a little bit of ancient history, and it is alive. In Ed Wood's refrigerator sit many quart-sized glass jars half full of a liquid, clear on the top with a settled, thick white layer below. When cold, the liquid gives no sign of life, but open a jar, add a little bit of the stuff to some flour and water, set it aside in a warm place, and a bubbling, growing, spongelike mass will rise up in the bowl. Added to more flour and water, allowed to rise a couple times, and then baked in a hot oven, this living scum will produce a delicious loaf of bread.

The jars in Wood's refrigerator are full of extraordinary microbes. They are a special combination of yeasts and lactobacilli that make up a sourdough starter. They make bread rise.

Wood has collected sourdough starters from all around the world. One particular starter, perhaps his most prized, was taken from a bakery in Giza, Egypt, that sits, as he says, "in the shadow of the pyramids." Here in Egypt, some five thousand years ago, humans most likely first learned to enlist microbes in creating the bread we know today. Once stranded in this fertile strip between deserts, the microbes in Wood's starter could in fact be the descendants of those very creatures. This living connection to history is only one of the reasons that Wood and others like him are so passionate about what Wood calls "real bread."

Some breads—for example, matzos, the unleavened crackers eaten at Jewish Passover; chapatis, the simple flour-and-water disks cooked over a fire in India; and Mexican tortillas—do not involve the work of microbes. For the first several thousand years that humans ate grains, the closest they came to bread were flat cakes made from a pastelike mixture of roasted grains and water that was spread over hot stones and cooked. The Greeks used to roll this bread up like a scroll to store it. This was all the bread the world knew until sometime about six thousand years ago, when leavened bread was born. Leavened, or raised, bread is the bread we are used to. It is a lacy arrangement of layers of dough that have caught the breath of microorganisms. The microbes feed hungrily on the dough's sugars and release carbon dioxide—the same gas we breathe out—as they transform the sugar into energy, then finally meet their death in the oven. The gas they have expelled lifts the dough into an airy structure unlike any flat bread ever eaten.

No one knows who first captured microbes to make bread rise, but most evidence indicates that it was probably an Egyptian baker who made the discovery by happy accident. The baker could have fallen asleep while the dough sat out in the kitchen, or perhaps he left some dough sitting overnight. There are many yeasts that live around us at

Egyptians carrying cone-shaped ceremonial loaves of bread, from the wall of a tomb in Egypt circa 2575 B.C.

all times. Yeast is a fungus, a member of the same group of organisms as mushrooms and bread mold, but, unlike its more expansive relatives, yeast is made up of one-celled creatures, tiny balls that are much too small to see. Yeast cells could easily drift into a dish of dough left sitting out on a counter overnight.

Yeast cells love sugar, and when they eat it, two things happen: they grow and reproduce, and they release carbon dioxide. Yeast cells reproduce by budding, which means another, smaller yeast cell grows right out of the side of its parent cell. In about an hour, the new cell is the same size as its parent cell, and in about an hour and fifteen minutes, both the parent and the child have started their own new little buds. At this rate, in ten hours, just one yeast cell has become one thousand cells, and in twenty hours it has become one million. All of those cells growing through-out the dough, and exhaling carbon dioxide into it, will cause the dough to puff up like a sponge.

Yeast cells will do one other thing when they eat sugar: if there is not enough oxygen available to make carbon dioxide, they will turn the sugar into alcohol. This is how yeast turns grape juice into wine and grain into beer. Even before they learned how to leaven bread, the Egyptians knew how to brew beer. It could be that the happy accident that led to leavened bread involved an Egyptian baker who found himself short of clean water and decided to throw some beer into the dough instead. In doing so, he may have given his dough a healthy dose of yeast: when the yeast cells grew, they puffed the dough up.

However it came about, the result was pleasant enough that eventually it was re-created on purpose again and again, and soon the word *bread* meant this mixture of microbes and water and flour. By the year 2000 B.C., there were professional bakers in Egypt and bread had become central to society. Wages were paid in bread: those who built the pyramids earned three loaves of bread and two jugs of beer a day. (All of their pay was in yeast products!) And as the passion for bread spread throughout the ancient world, the stuff that became known as the staff of life often gained spiritual significance as well. The Greeks had a festival of bread each fall. Roman bakers, the men who transformed flour and water into the tangy and airy delight of

A nearly two-thousand-year-old loaf of bread found in an oven in Pompeii, Italy. The eruption of Mount Vesuvius in the year A.D. 79 preserved the city of Pompeii even as it killed the inhabitants. Now excavated, Pompeii teaches us how people lived in the Roman Empire. Roman loaves of bread were often round like this one, or square, and baked with notches on top. The Egyptians most often made their loaves in a triangular shape

bread, were considered so special, so sacred even, that they were not allowed to participate in the vulgar entertainments of the masses: they were not allowed to go to see the gladiators fight or to even socialize with entertainers. It is not surprising that in this climate would arise a religious faith—Christianity—in which the central ritual is the eating of bread.

Even as hundreds of years later Roman bakers perfected the science of baking, and still hundreds more years later medieval bakers formed cooperative ovens, no one had any idea that bread was the work of a microbe. The Egyptians thought that something from their gods came into the dough and made it rise. They carefully kept a bit of dough from each batch to mix with the new dough and so impart to it the gift from the gods. This practice is exactly how bakers use sourdough starters today, but their reason for keeping that bit of dough for the next batch is completely different.

It was in 1680 that Antony van Leeuwenhoek, the Dutch microscopist, first recorded his observations of yeast, but it was another 150 years before scientists began to understand that yeast was responsible for bread and beer. It was the French scientist Louis Pasteur who finally proved this fungus's contribution.

Louis Pasteur shares with the German scientist Robert Koch the honor of being called a father of the modern study of microbes. In the second half of the nineteenth century these two men changed people's understanding of the world by proving convincingly the role of microbes in both baking and brewing—and in causing disease.

Louis Pasteur

Neither Pasteur nor Koch started out to study microbes: until they did their work, no one knew how to study microbes. Pasteur began his work in science as a chemist. Because people thought that the transformation of sugar to alcohol was purely a chemical reaction, it was to Pasteur that the head of a distillery in the French town of Lille came when he found that strange flavors were making their way into the alcohol he was making from beet sugar. Pasteur had certainly been thinking about this issue before he was approached. On the notes for a class he was teaching at the university he had scribbled: "What fermentation consists of. Mysterious character of the phenomenon." He began to work on the distiller's problem with great gusto, setting up a laboratory in the distillery basement. His wife wrote in a letter at the time: "Louis . . . is up to his neck in beet juice. He spends his days in an alcohol factory."

Pasteur examined the alcohol with the tools of the time and found that some of the compounds in it were chemicals that he was convinced could have been produced only by a living organism. So the chemist Pasteur found himself hot on the trail of a tiny living creature that might be in the distiller's product. Into his chemistry lab, among his flasks and beakers, he brought a microscope. Others had found yeast in beer and wine, and a few scientists had suggested it might be responsible for fermentation, but they were not taken seriously by those who believed in chemistry. However, when Pasteur saw round yeast cells in the alcohol at the plant, he was convinced these creatures acted as "alcohol factories" in the distiller's product. And he went on to prove it.

Through excruciatingly careful observations combining data from the microscope with recordings of the chemical composition of the fermenting sugar, Pasteur established convincingly that the alcohol was produced by yeast. He described observing in his laboratory, starting on December 10, 1858, yeast fermenting sugar into alcohol. He recorded the fine stream of bubbles he saw rising from a bit of yeast lying at the bottom of a flask, as well as how the amount of yeast and how quickly the cells multiplied related to the amount of alcohol that was produced in the flask. The yeast cells were not merely bystanders; they were intimately involved with the production of the alcohol.

In a very short time following Pasteur's finding, scientists managed to discover how to isolate yeast cells and then grow entire colonies—millions of cells exactly like the original one. When mixed among many other yeast cells, all grown from a mix of yeasts that fell from the air, one individual cell might not stand out. But when one cell could be isolated, and allowed to make precise copies of itself, a yeast could really display its talents. By doing this, scientists were able to find a yeast that grew faster than others, or fermented more quickly, and to breed that yeast for baking.

The commercial production of yeast in the United States was pioneered in the 1860s by brothers Charles and Maximillian Fleischmann, who immigrated from Austria-Hungary. Legend has it that their yeast business began when the two brothers arrived in New York to attend their sister's wedding and were so appalled at the poor quality of the available bread that one brother returned to his home country and came back with a vial of yeast in his shirt pocket.

Whatever the inspiration, the Fleischmann brothers quickly developed a process to create compressed cakes of yeast that could be sold to customers. Before yeast cakes became available, people simply saved bits of dough from one batch to "start" yeast growing in a new batch, or they let

A French bakery circa 1499. The baker slides the loaves back into the large wood-burning oven using a long-handled wooden peel. Not every home could afford a large oven, so people generally brought their dough to the town baker, who baked their loaves for a fee. It was not a trouble-free arrangement. Some worried that the baker would steal bits of their dough for his own loaves. The size of the loaves varied with how well they rose, so who could tell how much dough was used?

water mixed with potatoes or flour sit out until it caught yeast from the environment and began to bubble, or they added yeast left over from brewing.

The yeast the Fleischmanns produced was all one species called *Saccharomyces cerevisiae*, a type of yeast known for its reliable, fast-rising powers. It was about to take over the baking world. A baker could simply buy a foil-wrapped package of yeast and mix it into his dough. Refrigerated, the yeast would last a week.

The Fleischmanns and their business partners had so much faith in their idea that just a few years after their arrival in the United States they had built a giant compressed-yeast factory outside Cincinnati, Ohio. Bakers, however, were slow to become convinced of this new way to make bread. Thinking maybe the folk of a bigger city would be more open-minded, the Fleischmanns opened a second operation in New York City. Still no luck. They could make a lot of compressed yeast, but not many people wanted to buy it—they kept on just using the "free" yeast caught from the environment or saved in leftover dough. Losing money and desperate, the Fleischmanns decided to take their yeast to the 1876 Centennial Exposition being held in Philadelphia to celebrate the country's one hundredth birthday. There in the Vienna Bakery exhibition they demonstrated their yeast and served fresh-baked bread, coffee, ices, and chocolate. A reporter described their exhibit: "The Vienna Bakery is an establishment which cannot be too highly praised, and if its existence at the

Centennial should do what it promises, it may effect a permanent improvement in American breadmaking."

In fact, in the twenty years following the expo, the Fleischmanns did improve, or at least permanently change, the way Americans made bread. The business took off. Their yeast, formerly delivered door-to-door by a man carrying a basket, now began to be distributed by a fancy horse-drawn wagon advertising the product on its side. The challenge was to get this perishable product to customers quickly. Their slogan was "In storm, in sunshine, rain or sleet, you see our wagons on the street." No weather was too daunting for the "Fleischmann Man": no family need go without their yeast.

By 1900 the company, called simply Fleischmann's, had three plants; by 1925 it had twelve. In the largest, located in Peekskill, New York, thirty-six thousand pounds of yeast were manufactured daily. Thirty thousand bakers and 225,000 grocers received regular deliveries of yeast from Fleischmann's. In the early 1930s the company built a new research plant in the Bronx to explore new frontiers in yeast.

Fleischmann's also explored new ways to promote the use of its yeast. It started an "Eat More Bread" campaign featuring the character "John Dough." But this innovative company saw no reason to stop there: in the aftermath of World War I, while the country struggled with food short-

A full-page Fleischmann's advertisement, written as if it were an article, from a 1920s edition of the *Literary Digest*

The Glorious Art of Being Well

How thousands conquered their ills – found again the energy of youth — *with one fresh food*

Not a "cure-all," not a medicine in any sense— Fleischmann's Yeast is simply a remarkable fresh food.

The millions of tiny active yeast plants in every cake invigorate the whole system. They aid digestion—clear the skin—banish the poisons of constipation. Where cathartics give only temporary relief, yeast strengthens the intestinal muscles and makes them healthy and active. And day by day it releases new stores of energy.

Eat two or three cakes regularly every day before meals: on crackers—in fruit juices, water or milk—or just plain, nibbled from the cake. *For constipation especially, dissolve one cake in hot water (not scalding) before breakfast and at bedtime.* Buy several cakes at a time— they will keep fresh in a cool dry place for two or three days. All grocers have Fleischmann's Yeast. Start eating it today!

And let us send you a free copy of our latest booklet on Yeast for Health. Health Research Dept. A-79, The Fleischmann Company, 701 Washington St., New York.

"MY SKIN BROKE OUT in ugly blotches. Eating irregularly caused stomach trouble. Then I became constipated. One day a friend advised Fleischmann's Yeast. I started to eat it that day. In a month's time I was a new person. Every blemish had vanished from my skin. My eyes sparkled. My appetite was excellent. All as the result of Fleischmann's Yeast."

ETHEL PATRICK, Boston, Mass.

RIGHT

"AN ATHLETE and former physical director of the Cincinnati Gymnasium, during the war I served as director of an analine dye plant. When I returned to my old active work, I was not fit; I suffered from an acid stomach. Then I discovered Fleischmann's Yeast. I no longer suffer from acidity of the stomach . . . And I enthusiastically recommend Yeast to the men who come to me to be kept fit." FRANK MILLS, Cincinnati, Ohio

"AFTER A WINTER spent in the constant social activities of New York, I found myself in a seriously run-down condition. I was nervous and irritable. Dinners, dances, the theatre were a drudgery. I was completely worn out. A friend noticing my condition advised Fleischmann's Yeast. I began by eating three cakes a day, one before each meal. To my surprise, I soon felt noticeably better. My condition steadily improved. Now, thanks to Fleischmann's Yeast, I can dance all night and still feel fine the next day."

NATHALIE TRAVERS, New York City

THIS FAMOUS FOOD tones up the entire system—aids digestion—clears the skin—banishes constipation. You will find many delicious ways of eating Yeast: on crackers—in fruit juices, water or milk—with a little salt or just plain, nibbled from the cake. Eat two or three cakes regularly every day before meals.

ages, Fleischmann's promoted eating yeast itself, straight up, as a great source of nutrition! If eaten regularly, went the claim, yeast cakes could relieve constipation, skin problems, and a "run-down" feeling, among other things. Ads in newspapers and magazines featured personal testimonials by people (usually young women) for whom yeast changed their lives, and/or doctors with authoritative titles proclaiming the wonders of yeast for conquering "intestinal fatigue." These ads were printed in such a way that they looked just like another article rather than an advertisement. After only three years of this campaign, sales of Fleischmann's yeast increased by 130 percent and Fleischmann's was one of the top ten advertisers in magazines across the country.

World War II inspired Fleischmann's next big innovation. In laboratories in the Bronx, the company's researchers developed a dry form of yeast for use by the armed forces. This yeast did not need refrigeration and could remain active for years in its little foil packet. The yeast had been dried into dormancy, becoming similar to the spores of the Roquefort mold. In this slowed-down form of life, it did not grow and didn't need to eat or drink. Give this dried yeast a splash of warm water, however, and it sprang to life. It was not hard to imagine how this yeast could be handy for household as well as military use: no longer did you need to buy yeast each week. After the war the product was marketed to housewives as the best way to prevent "baking emergencies." In the early 1980s Fleischmann's improved on the product yet again, using new genetic techniques to produce a quick-rising yeast that worked 50 percent faster than the standard kind.

With the introduction of this product, baking was completely transformed from the process it had been just a hundred years before. The age-old way of baking, using leftover dough as a starter, could take almost twenty-four hours. In the traditional and popular French leavening process, one would take some starter, mix it with flour and water, and leave it to sit for a couple of hours in a warm place, giving the microbes a chance to wake up, start eating, and reproduce. Then it would be time to give them some more food, nearly twice as much flour and water this time, then let them work on that for a good eight hours, always, of course, in a warm area that was a "comfortable" temperature for them. Now it would be time to add more food again, this time more than twice as much as before, and let that digest for two more hours before adding the last and largest amount of water and flour, letting the dough rise for another half hour, forming it into loaves, letting them rise for a further four to five hours, and finally baking the bread!

In contrast, using "active dry" baking yeast, a baker could open a package of yeast and pour its 130 billion cells into some warm water. The bubbles they would send to the top would quickly signal they were getting ready to raise the dough. The baker could add flour and water to this yeast, let it rise for about an hour, shape it into loaves, let it rise for another hour, and be ready to bake. Suddenly, baking had gone from a twenty-four-hour process with many steps along the way, to a three-hour process that could be tucked into an afternoon.

But there were some problems with all this use of commercial yeast. *Saccharomyces cerevisiae* was a fantastic gas producer and so a great yeast for getting things done, but it was only one of hundreds of species of yeast, all of which had their own unique qualities capable of giving bread special flavors and textures. Other yeasts would have to take a backseat to the one yeast that had caught everyone's attention. And, in all the rush to get the bread baked already, one organism was being completely left behind, the unsung partner lurking in bread dough, the lactobacillus. The lactobacilli are small, single-celled creatures that have the rounded-off rectangular shape scientists refer to as a rod. They tend to line up in chains, end-to-end, like tiny boxcars. Common in cheese, yogurt, and sauerkraut, lactobacilli are found living in our mouths and intestines. They eat sugar and release lactic acid, giving yogurt and sourdough bread their tang. A package of commercial yeast cannot help but be contaminated by lactobacilli, as these organisms are everywhere, but in bread dough raised by commercial yeast the lactobacilli have very little time to reproduce before their lives end in the oven. This bread has none of the tang of sourdough, or its legendary ability to last.

One remarkable thing about the team of yeast and lactobacillus that can be seen in Ed Wood's refrigerator is that, unlike so many other things that live in the back of refrigerators, these jars of liquid do not change colors, grow fur,

Ed Wood's jars of culture, this one from Russia. The jar on the left shows how the culture appears sitting in his fridge. The middle jar has flour added: the foamy bubbles are signs of the yeast springing into action, eating, breathing, and reproducing. The culture on the right has settled down once more

and begin to send out plumes of stench every time the door is opened. It is not that no microbes grow in this nutritious combination of flour and water; on the contrary, these starters are little gardens of microbes, containing millions of microbes in each drop. But the microbes growing in sourdough starters are remarkably effective at keeping other microbes from getting a foothold—*Penicillium roqueforti*, the mold that will happily grow on a slice of bread, for instance. Ed Wood's sourdough starters, despite having lived with him for decades (far longer than any piece of bread could possibly last), resist invasion.

It is the way sourdough starters remain pristine that earned them their name. The word *sourdough* is a purely American invention that was given to these starters in the middle of the nineteenth century. Before then, they were simply called starters or leavens. In the mid-1800s the western United States was a frontier. The few people, few towns, and few bakeries that did exist there were separated by enormous wild spaces full of mountains and forests and deserts and—some thought—gold. In midcentury, word of gold to be panned from the streams or dug from the earth in the West brought a stream of prospectors to San Francisco and, later on, to Alaska. When they traveled out into the wilderness to seek their fortune, those prospectors had to carry on their backs all the food they needed. One very essential item was a ball of sourdough starter. This was long before the Fleischmanns invented active dry yeast. A starter carried in the top of a flour sack was the key to turning the contents of that sack from a dry dust to something with lightness and texture, a delicious and digestible food. The starters from San Francisco seemed to make a particularly tangy bread, so they were given the name sourdough.

The conditions for the miners were so severe, especially in Alaska, that having enough food and being able to both carry it and keep it edible became paramount. It was six hundred miles from the nearest town to the goldfields along the Klondike River in the Yukon. Fearing that gold-crazed prospectors would find themselves stranded and starving in the wilderness, Canada required each man heading out to the fields to carry a year's worth of food. The

Canadian Mounties set up scales where the trail to the goldfields crossed a narrow mountain pass, to make sure the miners carried at least three pounds of food per person per day into the wilderness. That meant each miner had to carry more than a thousand pounds of food in all. Beyond the scales, a line of prospectors snaked up a hillside as steep as a ski slope, pulling half a ton of gear each on sleds. Whatever they brought had to give them a great deal of nutrition per pound and be able to endure difficult travel and severe cold. Their mainstay was four hundred pounds of flour, and the best way to make this mostly flour diet palatable was a sourdough starter.

Tales abound of the care taken to keep a starter safe on the trail. Frontiersmen slept with the sourdough starter tucked into their sleeping bags at night to keep it from freezing in the bitter cold. One Alaskan sourdough cookbook writer claimed that when her husband built their first house, far off in the bush, he made a shelf near the stove for the sourdough pot even before he set up their bed. In time, the word *sourdough* came to refer not only to the tangy bread but also to the prospectors who carried it, and eventually came to refer to all the Alaskan pioneers: they were people who persisted—like sourdough—through all sorts of hard times.

These treasured frontier sourdough starters were sometimes passed down like family heirlooms, from generation to generation. Some are still being used to make bread today! In fact, one of the sourdough starters used by my neighborhood bakery in Seattle descended from a prospector. Knowing that, I get an extra kick from my sandwich. As my baker said, the yeast cells continually reproduce, so the starter is not really the same starter. Yet these microbe communities do have a sort of immortality, in that with proper care over the years, they continue to resist invasion by other species of microbes.

The unique tang and the persistence of the San Francisco sourdough eventually piqued the curiosity of food scientists. In 1970 a group from the University of California at Davis set out to discover what organisms created this remarkable bread. What they found was even more interest-

A typical miner's cabin in the Klondike. Above the seated miner's head is a large can of sourdough on the "kitchen" shelf

ing than they had hoped. In dough from five different bakeries in five different parts of San Francisco, in addition to the yeast *Candida milleri* there lived a microbe that had never before been identified. This microbe was clearly related to the lactobacilli but was different enough to be considered its own species: rather than forming neat little trains of boxcars, these microbes tended to clump together and take on strange shapes. And, unlike other lactobacilli, they needed one particular sugar to grow well.

Some of the reasons that this yeast and this special lactobacillus were found together in all the bread dough became clear upon further investigation. These microbes were like Jack Sprat and his wife: what one could eat, the other could not. The yeast did not eat one of the sugars released from the bread flour in the dough. It just so happened that this sugar, known as maltose, is just the one the lactobacillus needs to survive. Not only that, but the lactobacillus produces an antibiotic that kills the many other organisms that might invade the dough, but does not kill *Candida milleri*. Thus the lactobacillus keeps the dough safe for just itself and its partner. And, although many microbes cannot tolerate the acids released by the lactobacilli, this particular type of yeast grows quite well in an acidic environment. In honor of this special lactobacillus's role in creating San Francisco's special sourdough bread, the scientists named their new find *Lactobacillus sanfrancisco*.

Although the San Francisco culture has perhaps been studied the most, it is known that all sourdough cultures consist of a marriage of between one or more types of lactobacillus and one or more types of yeast. The type of bacillus and the type of yeast vary, but all starters arise from this happy union. As a result, not only do starter cultures persist and resist invasion but the work of these organisms also creates a bread that both resists the growth of mold after it is baked and takes longer than other breads to become stale. Although all the microbes in the bread dough are killed in

HOW TO HARNESS A WILD YEAST

Want to try to make your own sourdough culture using the yeast and lactobacilli that live around you? The process is simple, but success is not guaranteed, and may take patience and persistence.

• *Step 1:* In a large, clean bowl, using a clean spoon, combine 1 cup wheat flour with 1 cup water. Mix well.

As you will be leaving this mixture to sit out for days, hoping the microbes you want will grow in it, it is best to start with a clean bowl and clean spoon and clean hands to avoid introducing microbes you do not want.

Some people claim the microbes you do want are more likely to grow if some of the flour you use is rye flour. Some claim the microbes need minerals found in the rye flour to eat; others say microbes travel on the flour itself. If you first try with wheat flour alone and have trouble, you might want to add some rye.

• *Step 2:* Cover the bowl with a clean kitchen towel, and let it sit in a warm spot (60–70 degrees Fahrenheit) for 2 days. Watch for the

the oven, the acids that they have produced in the bread slow the growth of mold and keep the bread fresh. And it is not just the acid: scientists studying sourdough bread have found that the lactobacilli in certain starters actually produce chemicals that kill mold. Although conventional bread may begin to mold in just two days, sourdough bread can last for seven days without molding.

---

appearance of little bubbles near the surface of the mixture. This is a sign that microbes have moved in and are growing in the mixture. Throw away any dried-out or crusty part of the mixture; then feed the mixture with another cup of flour and enough water to make a soft dough. Set aside, covered, for another day.

Some suggest using nonchlorinated water to avoid killing microbes. I have never had trouble using chlorinated tap water to grow baker's yeast when I make bread, but if you are having trouble, you could try uncarbonated bottled water.

• *Step 3:* Feed the mixture again each day for 2 more days until it is foamy and light, glossy and sweet-smelling. By the fifth day it should be "growing" about twice as fast. Now you are ready to use it to bake any recipe for sourdough bread. Be sure to save some in a jar in your refrigerator as your own wild sourdough starter!

If at any point your starter begins to smell bad, throw it out and start again. You may have to find a new place for it to sit, or make sure you have a clean bowl, spoon, hands, and towel. Do not give up—just try again.

These preservative powers make sourdough attractive not just to people who want to eat good bread but also to people in the bakery business who are interested in making long-lasting bread for a growing group of customers who don't like artificial preservatives.

It was the wonderful flavors produced by the mix of lactobacilli and yeast in sourdough that first sent Ed Wood out bioprospecting around the globe. Though not a baker by trade, Wood is uniquely able to appreciate sourdough bread. In his enthusiastic life he has studied fish in the Columbia River in the northwestern United States and attended medical school to become a pathologist, the detective type of doctor who examines samples from patients, looking for clues to their disease. He worked for the space program as part of the team that made certain the *Apollo 11* moon mission did not bring back strange microbes from space. Then, in 1983, he moved to Saudi Arabia to become the head pathologist at a new hospital there. Throughout these adventures, though, his other passion was bread. Wood loved to bake bread, and his training in pathology made him uniquely able to appreciate the special qualities of the microbes involved in sourdough.

Although many commercial bakeries in the United States resort to using commercial yeast so that their bread rises reliably and quickly, Wood believed that he would find in the bakeries of the Middle East a wide variety of breads raised with a starter. These starters, he believed, would consist of a special and stable marriage of microbes, a union of yeast and lactobacillus that got along well, kept out invaders, and produced good bread. And they just might be the descendants of the microbes used by the world's first bakers.

Ed Wood was convinced of something else as well: starters from different places in the world full of different microbes would all make unique bread. As more and more of the world picks up speed and has no time for twenty-four hours of bread making, these cultures might become obsolete. Wood decided they would not be lost if he could help it. Now he collects cultures, propagates them in his Idaho home, and sells them on the Internet. His Web site features fifteen different cultures originating everywhere from South Africa and Australia to the Yukon.

In the five thousand years that we have been using microbes to make bread, it is only in the past century and a half that we have even realized what we were doing. But the microbes, nevertheless, managed for all that time to get us to keep them fed, to save a little dough from each batch so they can go on proliferating, even to tuck them into our sleeping bags to keep them warm in the cold Alaskan night. And now it appears that we are even helping these microbes access the most modern means of dispersal: orders placed at Ed Wood's Web site send these microbes flying across the country and around the world. Perhaps this is the real perfect marriage, that of human and bread starter, devoted to each other for the past five thousand years.

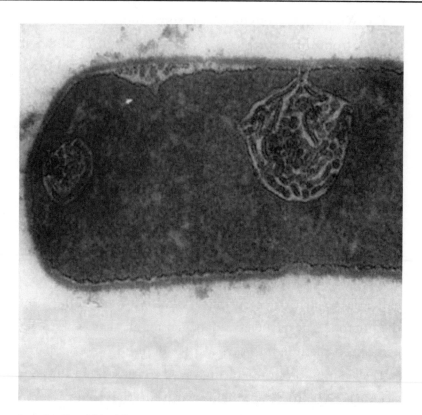

Lactobacillus acidophilus

Food of the Gods

The chief value of this cocoa is a beverage that they make called chocolate, which is prized to the point of folly in that land. It is nauseating to some who are not accustomed to it, for it has froth on top and a sort of lees [scum], which indeed require a good deal of effort to drink. Yet it is the most prized drink and is offered to noblemen as they pass through their lands. Both Indians and Spaniards, and especially Spanish women who have grown accustomed to the land, adore their black chocolate . . . Those who have not been brought up to it do not much care for it.

—SPANISH JESUIT JOSÉ DE ACOSTA IN 1590, ABOUT THE
    USE OF CHOCOLATE IN THE NEW WORLD

I was accustomed, even before I began to write this book, to think of the microbes that made my cheese. I was reminded of them by the white skins they wrapped around some cheeses and the holes they made in others. And, having made bread many times and watched the yeast bubble happily when mixed with warm water, I was used to thanking microbes for my toast. It never occurred to me, however, that chocolate, perhaps my all-time favorite food, was the product of microbes who had transformed the seed of the cacao tree into something delicious.

When Christopher Columbus made his fourth voyage of exploration of the New World, he was trying yet again to find the passage through or around the landmass of the Americas to finally reach the Far East. His goal was to secure for his sponsors, the king and queen of Spain, access to the gold and the valuable spices of the Far East. He set sail in May of 1502 with 150 men and four ships. Upon reaching the islands that dot the Caribbean, he sailed for Jamaica but missed it and anchored instead at the island of Guanaja off the coast of Honduras. There appeared in the waters an enormous dugout canoe, looking to be almost as long as the Spanish ship—nearly 150 feet long—and at least 8 feet wide, paddled by twenty-five men. Under a large shelter of palm leaves in the middle of the boat rode the passengers and piles of trade goods. Columbus ordered his men to seize the canoe, and the canoe's occupants complied, allowing themselves and a sampling of their goods to be taken aboard. The Spanish found no gold among the woven clothes, swords and hatchets, roots and grains, and corn wine, but they did find a great many small brown seeds, looking to the Spanish something like almonds:

These the Indians in the canoe valued greatly, for I noticed that when they were brought aboard with the other goods,

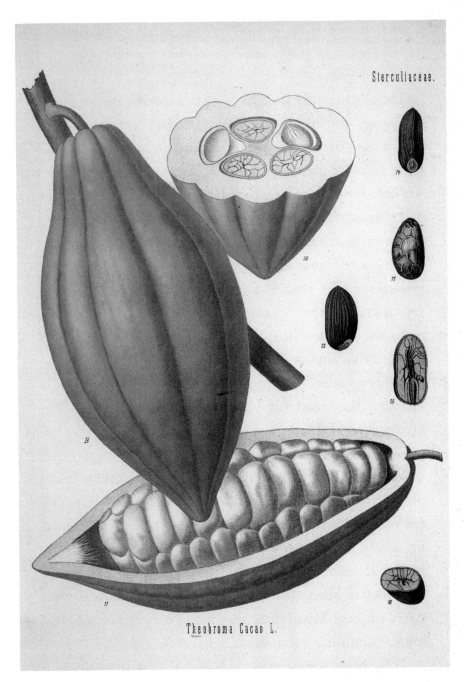

Theobroma cacao, the source of chocolate, from *A Modern Herbal*, 1931

*and some fell to the floor, all the Indians squatted down to
pick them up as if they had lost something of great value.*

These "almonds" were in fact cacao beans, the source of
chocolate, something no European had yet tasted. To
Columbus, they were forever to remain just the strange
trade goods of a strange people, of little value to him. Looking only for the treasures he was familiar with, such as gold
and silver, he failed to see past the unassuming appearance
of the cacao beans. He sailed on, searching for the passage
to the eastern lands and their rumored gold and spices. He
was to die four years later, never having tasted the marvelous product those beans could produce.

To the people of the New World, including the Mayan
people who almost certainly paddled the trading canoe
Columbus raided, the product of the cacao bean was so valued that they used the beans themselves as money. One
hundred cacao beans was a porter's wages for a day, an
amount he could trade for a turkey hen or a jackrabbit. A
turkey egg could be had for three beans, as could a fresh-
picked avocado or a meal of fish wrapped in cornhusks. The
Spanish explorers did not come to understand cacao's worth
for nearly twenty more years, not until the conquistadors
led by Hernán Cortés invaded the Yucatán peninsula and
the valley of Mexico. In the storehouses of the palace of the
Aztec emperor Montezuma they found not piles of gold but
some 960 million cacao beans.

These beans were not just money—they were money you
could eat. Cacao beans could be made into the nutritious

and much-longed-for *chocolatl*. This rich drink was really a food: it resembled a soup or a gruel more than a beverage. *Chocolatl* was made of cacao beans that had been ground into powder and then mixed with water. This mixture was then beaten and poured back and forth between containers until it was foamy. Because the beans were used whole, the drink contained all their fat, making it more like drinking a melted chocolate bar than what we know as cocoa. But since it was most often unsweetened and somewhat coarse, imagine a melted, bitter, gritty chocolate bar. The Mayans served it hot and were known to add vanilla beans as well as pieces of an ear-shaped flower from a relative of the custard-apple tree, which added a peppery flavor to the drink. They also made a hot gruel of cacao, corn, and water.

The Aztecs, in contrast, drank their *chocolatl* cold, sometimes sweetened with honey (there was no cane sugar in the Americas until Europeans brought it). They also added ground hot chili, achiote—a seed that adds a bright red color and a somewhat bitter flavor—and many different tropical flowers for flavoring. It was considered very nutritious.

And as you might imagine of a refreshment that was actually made of money, this drink was reserved for the wealthy. Even those who could afford it saved it for special occasions and ceremonies. Spanish explorers describe observing the Aztec emperor having *chocolatl* at a banquet. Although the feast consisted of more than three hundred dishes, he ate sparingly of the food but downed cup after cup of the drink, served in what one writer called "cups of fine gold." (This may have been the Spaniards' wishful

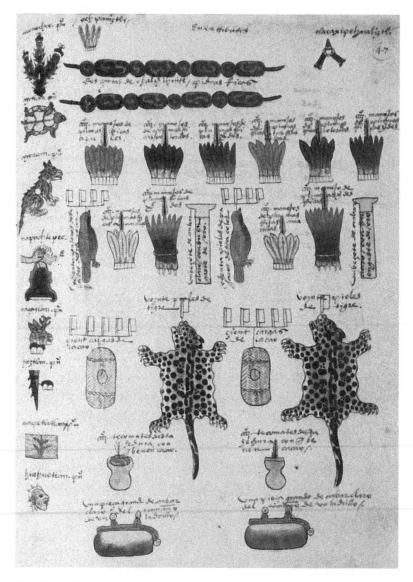

The *Códice Mendoza* from the 1500s shows what the people of a region in what is now Mexico had to give to their Aztec rulers in tax. The tax included jaguar skins, feathers from the cotinga bird, a green stone that was considered very valuable, and 200 loads of cacao as well as 800 gourds with which to drink *chocolatl*

thinking, as another witness said the cups were in fact pieces of gourd called calabash.)

The Mayan people also used cacao ceremoniously. Babies were ritually anointed with cacao on their faces and between their fingers and toes. Cacao was an important part of courtship ceremonies among those who could afford it. It was offered to gods in religious ceremonies, and when the wealthy were buried with their jaguar-pelt robes and jade jewelry, they were accompanied into the afterlife by pots full of cacao.

At first the charms of this beverage were not appreciated by the Spanish newcomers, such as the Jesuit whose quote begins this chapter. The Spanish chronicler Girolamo Benzoni was also slow to be won over. He wrote in his *History of the New World* (1565):

> *[Cacao seems] more suited for pigs than for men. I was upwards of a year in that country without ever being induced to taste this beverage; and when I passed through a tribe, if an Indian wished occasionally to give me some, he was very much surprised to see me refuse it, and went away laughing. But subsequently, wine failing, and unwilling to drink nothing but water, I did as others did. The flavour is somewhat bitter, but it satisfies and refreshes the body without intoxicating: the Indians esteem it above everything, wherever they are accustomed to it.*

Eventually, all of Europe was to have a similar transformation. By 1753 the Swedish botanist Linnaeus named the cacao tree *Theobroma*—"food of the gods" in Latin.

It is hard to fault Columbus for not realizing that the unassuming seeds he saw were the source of the food of the gods. In fact, it is astonishing that anyone ever comprehended the value of these seeds. Chocolate emerges from a humble cacao bean through a process so complex and mysterious it is a wonder that this remarkable flavor was ever discovered.

The cacao tree can grow only in the heat of the tropics. The tree is native to the rain forest; at thirty feet tall it still grows in the shade of the towering trees that make up the uppermost reaches of the forest canopy. The first signs of the chocolate to come are the tiny flowers of this tree, no bigger than a nickel yet a very complex, orchid-like bloom. Strangely, the blooms spring straight from the trunk and branches of the tree, in dense clusters, as many as six thousand per tree. They range in color from whitish pink to whitish yellow. Each lasts only a day, opening around sunrise. Before the sun sets that day, the blossom must be found by a tiny insect known as a midge, a creature no bigger than the head of a pin. This midge is small enough to navigate the tight passageways into the center of the flower and pollinate it. But of all the blooms on the tree, as few as one in one hundred will be pollinated before they close that night, and the next day the blooms will fall to the ground, their chance of being transformed into cacao fruits past.

The *Códice Tudela* from the 1500s depicts a Mexican woman making a chocolate drink frothy by pouring it back and forth between two cups

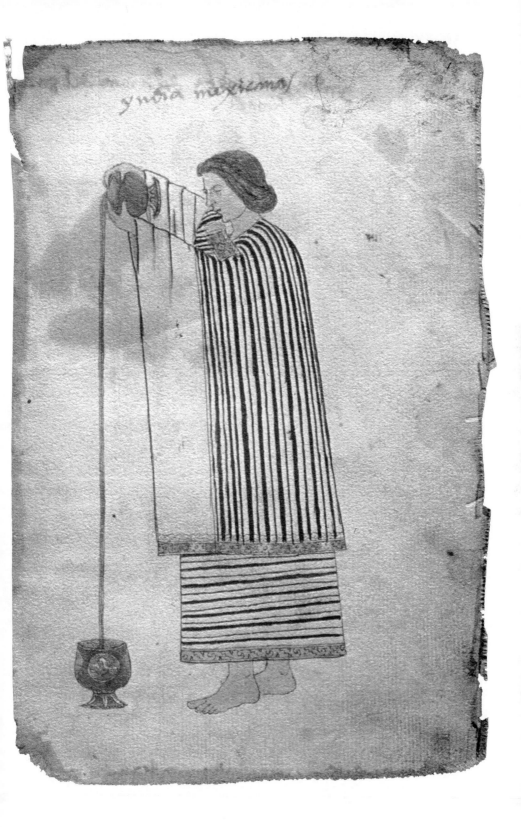

Of those blossoms that are pollinated, only about twenty to forty will mature into fruits. The cacao fruit is an elongated pod the shape and size of a small football. Some pods are smooth, some bumpy, some ridged, depending on the species. Because they grow directly from the pollinated blossom, they, too, sprout straight from the trunk and the branches. This seemed so odd to European illustrators that they sometimes disbelieved eyewitness accounts of the tree and just drew the fruits on branches, as an apple or a peach would grow. As the fruit ripens, it changes from green to red and finally to orange. Five to six months after the blossom's encounter with the midge, the fruit is ready to harvest. When split open, it will reveal sweet white pulp wrapped around about thirty pale, almond-sized seeds.

One can easily imagine that the people living in the jungles where the cacao tree grew would be attracted to the pulp of this fruit, given that it was eaten with great relish by climbing mammals such as monkeys and squirrels. All one had to do was open a ripe pod to enjoy the succulent flesh. The seeds, however, were another matter. For the cacao tree, whose pods do not open of themselves to disperse seeds, having an animal open the pods and eat the flesh was a convenient way to have its progeny dispersed. But if the animal were to chew up the seeds, that would be a problem: chewed-up seeds would not become cacao trees. Probably the cacao's continued survival depended on the fact that its seeds were strikingly bitter and sour and not at all appealing to eat.

It is the seeds' off-putting taste that makes it seem unlikely that anyone ever thought to do the following: split open the pods, scrape out the seeds and the pulp, and pile them in a heap covered with banana leaves. Left like this for several days, the pile becomes warmer and warmer, reaching 125 degrees Fahrenheit by day two. The pulp liquefies, leaving the seeds—damp, darker brown, and shriveled— with the embryo of the cacao tree dead inside them. The wet seeds then must be dried for a couple of days by being spread in the sun and continually turned, raked, and moved out of the rain if necessary so they do not rot. Now, after all of this, the seeds begin to taste something like the bitterest of chocolate.

Cacao beans drying in the sun on pieces of sheet metal in a Mayan village in the Toledo district of Belize. The tropical forests of this Central American country are the perfect place for cacao to grow

What is the key to the transformation of these bitter seeds to the much-valued concoction we know as chocolate? While piled in a heap on the floor of the rain forest, the fruits of the cacao tree are devoured by a series of ravenous microorganisms who in the process manage to completely transform the seed itself. The microbes work like a symphony orchestra: first one type rises in prominence and, having done its part, recedes, while the next group takes over. But this symphony must play without a conductor— it is the changes that occur in the fermenting cacao fruit itself that signal the changes of the players.

The first group to dominate is the yeasts. Yeasts can rap-

CHOCOLATE AND THE RAIN FOREST

Two-thirds of the world's cacao is now grown in West Africa, most of it by small farmers. These farmers originally planted cacao like any other crop, cutting down the forest and replacing it with fields of just cacao trees in hopes of selling the beans for a living. For a few years, such plantations will produce a fair amount of cacao. But after that the trees bear fewer and fewer fruits. Eventually, they sicken. Out in the hot sun, in an open field, is not how a cacao tree likes to grow. Even the most robust species of cacao cannot thrive in such a field. The cacao tree needs the shade of taller trees to protect it. Its pollinating midge needs the rubbish on the forest floor to live in.

The silver lining in the hardships experienced by cacao farmers

idly change sugar to energy even in the dense, airless confines of a sweet pulpy pile. They quickly outgrow the other
organisms and dominate the heap. They also break down
the hard outer coating of the seeds, allowing the bitter
chemicals trapped inside to leak out. Yeasts feeding on
sugar in the pile of cacao fruit produce alcohol, and soon a
drunken smell wafts through the cacao patch. Eventually,
the yeast cells are pickled in their own alcohol and die. In
their place, in the heap now warmed from the activity of so
many organisms, emerge the microbes that feed happily on
alcohol—our old friends the lactobacilli. These creatures
change the pulp into an acidy soup: the white flesh of the

---

is that by planting cacao in a mixed plot—that is, among taller shade
trees, and with smaller trees around them—they can grow healthy
crops of cacao and also preserve some of the diversity of the rain
forest. Maintaining this diversity preserves not only the many species
that depend on that environment all year long but also some species
that spend much of the year in other parts of the world. Songbirds
that travel south in the winter need the shady mixed ecology of the
rain forest as a winter home. Mixed cacao plantations can keep them
alive through the winter and so keep them singing in northern yards
and parks in the spring. And there is another benefit to this type of
cacao field: it allows farmers to plant less hardy but better-tasting
cacao, which makes better-tasting chocolate.

fruits becomes a clear liquid, a cacao vinegar. When the processors drain this off and stir the beans, the next group of bugs moves to the fore, the acetic acid bacteria, who use the oxygen stirred into the drier, looser mound of beans to finish the fermentation.

The time it takes to complete the fermentation process depends on the species of the bean, only two days for some and as long as six for others. When samples of beans are cut open, and the tree embryo within the seed is appropriately

A Mayan woman preparing a drink from cacao beans. She has ground the dried beans on her concave grinding stone, called a *metate*, using her cylindrical stone pestle. This is the same tool used by the Maya for centuries to grind cacao

shriveled, the beans are turned out and spread to dry. If the beans are not dried, the organisms can begin to break down the embryo itself and fungi can begin to grow, adding their rich, but not necessarily desirable, flavors.

How do all of these microorganisms get into the ripening heap? The reader who has been reading this book from the beginning can probably make a pretty good guess at the answer to that question, but the reader who has skipped ahead to dessert may need a few clues. Until recently, very little was known about the succession of microbes that act on cacao, but experiments done in the early 1970s found that the fruits themselves were sterile—free from microbes—before they were opened. Yeasts, however, the primary players in the fermentation cascade, were found in abundance on the hands of the harvesters. Also, many of the microbes involved were found in the boxes used over and over for fermentation. These pockets of microbes acted like a sourdough starter to get the fermentation brewing.

The beans must be fermented and dried on the tropical plantations where they grow. Then these transformed beans are taken to chocolate factories around the world to be roasted, ground, mixed with sugar and flavorings like vanilla, ground further into a powder, kneaded for three days or longer, heated, poured into molds, cooled, and wrapped up as a chocolate bar. (To make cocoa, some of the roasted and ground beans would be pressed to remove the fat, producing pure cocoa butter as well.)

Microbes have transformed this bad-tasting seed into a food called worthy of the gods, a food so desired it was once used as money and has now been carried by human beings all over the world and planted in more than thirty countries. More than one million tons of chocolate are produced each year. Whole institutes are devoted to treating diseases of the cacao tree.

Chocolate is very important to me, and now when I eat it (almost every day) I thank the microbes that it exists. But for most people in the world chocolate is not such an important food. In fact, 90 percent of the world's chocolate is eaten in Europe and the Americas. These are also the parts of the world most likely to serve cheese at lunch. In Asia and Africa (and among people in Europe and the Americas who follow Asian and African eating traditions) cheese, chocolate, and bread are not often on the menu. But there are many, many other foods created by microbes that are.

The forty-five million people who live in South Korea, and Korean emigrants around the world, are all hoping to sit down to a lunch that includes kimchi, a flavorful dish that is something like a spicy pickle. Although this dish, made of fermented vegetables or meat, is only a side dish, never the main course, it is important to Koreans. In fact, a Korean saying goes, "Without kimchi on the table, the stomach feels as if nothing had been eaten at all." Kimchi found its way into the Korean diet as an excellent way to preserve vegetables through the harsh Korean winter, in the days before supermarkets and vegetables shipped in from warmer parts of the world. The process of salting the vegetables and allowing them to ferment keeps them crisp and full of vitamins. There are more than one hundred

Peter's Chocolate

The ideal food for mountain climbing, or for any out-of-door exercise, or for any exercise anywhere—or as a food any time you are hungry.

Peter's has that truly delicious flavor that makes you always want more.

Peter's Milk Chocolate   *Peter's Almond Milk Chocolate*
Peter's Milk Chocolate Croquettes   *Peter's Bon-Bons*
Peter's Thimbles with Roasted Hazelnuts

An ad from the early twentieth century for a chocolate bar as a "wholesome" snack

types of kimchi made, some with vegetables, others with seafood. All involve a process of soaking the ingredients in salt and water, which prevents the growth of unwanted microbes that cannot tolerate the salt. At the same time, the salt leaches water and sugar out of the foods, encouraging the growth of lactobacilli, which transform the sugar into lactic acid, giving the food a pleasant sour bite and enough acidity to prevent other microbes from growing.

In the late fall, many Korean businesses give their employees "kimchi bonuses" to buy the ingredients to make kimchi for the winter. Korean refrigerators have a special

CHOCOLATE FOR THE PEOPLE

No Aztec emperor would recognize my chocolate bar as the same sacred food he drank in his ceremonial cup. In the late nineteenth and early twentieth centuries chocolate underwent almost as profound a transformation as that from cacao bean to *chocolatl*. In the first place, new technologies made it possible to create the smooth, creamy, milky substance we love in our candy. A Dutch chemist, by the name of Coenraad Johannes van Houten, learned how to take the fat out of chocolate and treat it with alkalizing agents, creating "cocoa," which mixed much better with water than the fatty product direct from the bean. Next, a Swiss man by the name of Rudolphe Lindt developed a way to mix chocolate called "conching" that left it very smooth. And, just as important as these developments, mass production made this product affordable for ordinary people.

kimchi storage compartment. And it is said that a woman is not suitable for marriage unless she can make at least twelve different kinds of kimchi.

About 250 million people in sub-Saharan Africa eat cassava for just about every meal, and as many as another 250 million in Asia, Latin America, and other parts of Africa depend on the crop for food or for their livelihood. This starchy root plant, something like a sweet potato, is easy to grow—one can produce a new cassava plant merely by cutting off a stem and sticking it in the ground—and a single plant can produce fifty pounds of food. Cassava grows well

Several of the big chocolate manufacturers, including Cadbury and Fry in England and Hershey in the United States, made their fortunes by turning out sweet chocolate candies for the masses and even created whole towns for their employees. In 1903 Milton S. Hershey bought a farm in southeastern Pennsylvania and built not only a chocolate factory but a department store, a bank, churches, a library, a hotel, schools, parks, a ballroom, a zoo, a stadium, an amusement park, and a school for orphan boys. Hershey named town streets Chocolate and Cocoa, as well as Caracas, Granada, and Aruba, after cities from which he bought his cacao beans. The streetlights were made in the shape of Hershey's chocolate-drop candies called Kisses.

The flood of visitors to this town, which advertises itself as "the Sweetest Place on Earth," caused the town to stop allowing factory tours, but there are plenty of other amusements that await twenty-in poor soil and can survive long periods of little rainfall. Left in the ground, the cassava root remains edible for as long as three years. In places where little else grows well, it can be a food factory.

But cassava has two rather serious drawbacks. First, within three days of being picked, unprotected cassava roots begin to rot into a jellylike mass. Second, and even more serious, when the cells of the plant are broken open— for instance, by someone taking a bite—the plant's juices start to form a poison known as cyanide. Eating enough cyanide could be deadly, and the more poorly nourished an individual is, the less poison is necessary to be fatal.

first-century tourists. You can stay at Hershey Lodge and have breakfast with people dressed as various Hershey products (such as a Reese's Peanut Butter Cup). Later, see these products come to life in a 3-D musical production. Spend a summer afternoon riding the world's first hydraulic-launch roller coaster at Hershey Park, which goes from 0 to 72 miles an hour in two seconds, then check in for chocolate spa treatments at the Hotel Hershey. (Choose between the Chocolate Escape: the Whipped Cocoa Bath, followed by the Chocolate Bean Polish, the Chocolate Fondue Wrap, and the Cocoa Massage; and the Hershey Peppermint Pattie, which features a Peppermint Salt Scrub, followed by the Chocolate Fondue Wrap.) And at Hershey's Chocolate World you can take a tour ride through a simulated factory and enjoy a free sample at the end.

Cyanide can save a crop from insects and animals that might otherwise devour it, but the plant can also be dangerous for the unwary human.

The solution? Fermentation produces cassava that will keep and is not deadly. In West Africa, cassava is grated, then put in sacks and pressed with weights for a few days. Together, the heat of the fermentation and the acid produced by the bacteria that grow in the plant preserve it and reduce the poison. The fermented cassava—called gari in West Africa—is dried, first in the sun and then in large skillets or ovens. The resulting food, which is granular like rice or couscous, feeds millions.

In addition to preserving foods for lean times, fermentation can transform things that were previously inedible and thereby help people create foods out of the most unlikely substances. In the Sudan, one of the hottest and driest countries in Africa, prone to drought and lately ravaged by civil war, both of which prevent farmers from growing food, over sixty different types of fermented foods are made and more than half of them are eaten during times of famine. In this harsh and uncertain environment, people have relied on microbes to turn the most unlikely things into nutritious food. Hides, hooves, gall bladders, fat, intestines, caterpillars, locusts, frogs, and cow urine are all made into food by fermentation in the Sudan.

Throughout China and Japan, and many countries in Southeast Asia, soy sauce is the accompaniment to every meal. This salty brown sauce with a distinctive meaty flavor is the product of a collaboration of molds, bacteria, and yeast feeding on a mixture of roasted soybeans and wheat. The molds required to start the fermentation can be caught by making apple-sized balls of steamed rice or soybeans, wrapping them in leaves, tying them tightly with string, and then hanging them in the shade of the eaves, where they are protected from rain but can catch the breeze. In a few months, when they are covered with the white strands of mold, they are taken down and put to use in a number of fermented foods.

One way to make soy sauce is to add mold spores to a mixture of cooked soybeans and roasted wheat. The mix is kept in a warm place for about three days and then poured into a barrel of salty water. Over the next twelve months, the mold spores, along with yeasts and bacteria, do their magic, turning this simple mixture into a very desirable condiment. Microbes can bring subtle flavors to soy sauce, as they do to cheese and to wine. Japan alone has more than twenty-five hundred small soy-sauce manufacturers who create very diverse flavors with their microbe collaborators.

Wherever sausage is being enjoyed as a part of lunch, the eaters owe their enjoyment to the work of microbes. Sausage is made from a mixture of meat, spices, and salt to which starter cultures of lactobacilli are added. Then the sausages are allowed to dry, during which time the acidity produced by the lactobacilli and the increasing saltiness and lack of water prevent the growth of microbes that would poison or destroy the meat.

Across southern India, eating means having *idli* or *dosa*, both created from combinations of ground rice and lentils, mixed with water and allowed to ferment. *Idli* are formed into balls and then steamed and served like dumplings, and *dosa* are pancakes made from this fermented mixture.

In Ethiopia, a meal is not considered complete without *injera.* Fermentation of the dough of the wheatlike grain *tef* creates this bread, which has the consistency of a spongy cloth and a mild, sour flavor. The bread is an edible utensil: in lieu of spoons, torn-off bits are used to pick up and eat mouthfuls of spicy stews.

In Scandinavian countries, a fermented fish might be part of lunch. This tradition arose in northern fishing communities as a way to preserve the catch through the long winter, when ice and cold would make fishing difficult if not impossible. Placed in pits in the ground covered with fir boughs, the fish soften and gain a distinctive flavor. The resulting dish is often completely disgusting to the uninitiated, who might react to it even more strongly than the Spanish did to chocolate upon first introduction, but those who have grown up eating it not only find the strong flavor appealing but also feel that this food signifies the uniqueness of their culture.

If you talk to friends and neighbors of different ethnic backgrounds, or explore the ethnic restaurants and stores in your town, you will find an endless array of the products of microbes. Coffee, tea, vanilla, olives, vinegar, and sauerkraut—just to name a few we have not even mentioned— all depend on fermentation. Microbes preserve our foods, making us able to eat through the winter and on long journeys. They keep us alive during famines; in some cases, like that of cassava, they transform foods from poisons to staples, and in others, like that of cacao, they turn icky seeds into the food of the gods. Microbes have created foods so powerful and unusual, like kimchi, that to eat them is to come home, to be a member of a particular group. Such foods have inspired festivals and museums and even poetry! They have also created an unending number of unusual flavors in food to explore and savor. What microbes have done for our meals before we eat them may only be surpassed by what microbes do for our meals once we swallow them.

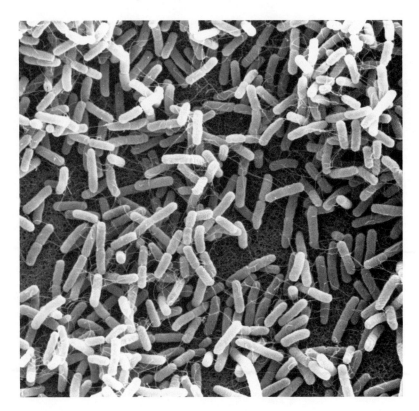

E. coli—the most populous microbe in our gut

Microbes Are Us

The human body is estimated to contain 10^{14} [a hundred trillion] cells, 10% of which belong to the body proper. The remaining 90% represent the population of organisms living in or on the host.
—Lora V. Hooper, Lynn Bry, Per G. Falk, and
  Jeffrey Gordon

As saturated with microbes as the cheese in our sandwich might be, and as crawling with yeast as the bread was before it was baked, that is nothing compared to the fun-house ride our meal begins as it enters our mouth. In our large intestine, the microbes grow thicker than in the blue rivers of mold in Roquefort. About one hundred trillion bugs make this organ their home, growing as dense as one hundred billion per quarter teaspoonful. As a matter of fact, if we were to consider our bodies as a mass of living cells, we would find that only a small percentage are human cells. As the quote that starts this chapter notes, 90 percent of the cells in and on our body belong to microbes.

Microbes move in as soon as we are born. If we are healthy, the pool of fluid in which we swim inside our mother's womb is microbe-free, but as soon as we break out of this bubble and begin to travel toward the outside world, microbes hop on. Anywhere hospitable is fair game. To a microbe, a small opening in our skin is the yawning mouth of a giant, welcoming cave. It is by venturing through these openings that microbes find some of their favorite spots—dark, warm, moist places that are perfect for raising their kids. Although they settle by the hundred on every square centimeter of our backs, and by the hundred thousand on each like-sized space on our scalps, one million occupy each square centimeter of our cozy armpits, and *one billion or more* live in each thimble-sized portion of our large intestine. It is this tube, the final digesting place of our food before it leaves our body as feces, that contains the great majority of our microbe residents.

On the way into our body, our cheese-sandwich-and-chocolate-bar lunch will briefly meet a good number of bugs in our mouth. In comparison, our acidic stomach will seem like a microbe wasteland. The small intestine—the twenty-foot-long tube that twists and coils away from the stomach—will house a few more bugs, but it is upon arrival at the five-foot-long large intestine that the real action begins.

Illustration of the intestines by the remarkable sixteenth-century anatomist Vesalius

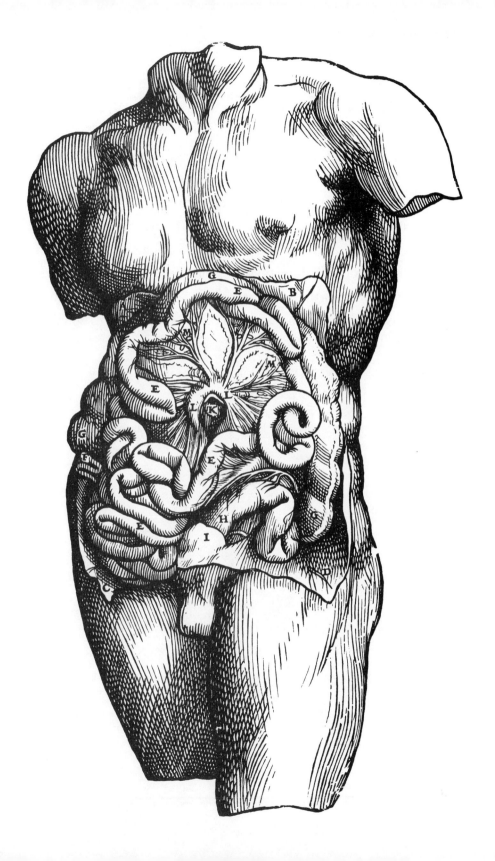

By the time it leaves our body, our meal, transformed into an unattractive remnant of itself, will be nearly two-thirds microbes by weight.

If the thought of all of these creatures teeming inside you gives you the creeps, you are not alone. From the time humans first began to understand that we share our bodies with these guests, opinions on their presence have varied from "They must be helpful" (Louis Pasteur, one of history's greatest microbiologists, who pioneered the scientific study of microbes in the mid-nineteenth century) to "They must be poisonous" (Elie Metchnikoff, a Nobel Prize–winning

Elie Metchnikoff

scientist a generation younger than Pasteur). And although we still have not reconciled ourselves to our invisible companions, we are finally beginning to understand some of their great contributions to our health. In some ways we are discovering that both Metchnikoff and Pasteur were right.

Metchnikoff (1845–1916) became so certain of the evils of the intestinal microbes that he devoted the last years of his career to finding a way to rid the bowels of them. Metchnikoff was a world-renowned scientist, and the excellence of his work had won him the position of director of the Pasteur Institute—named for Louis Pasteur. As he grew older, he began to look into the mirror with horror: he was aging, his life was passing, and he didn't want to die. Rather than accepting this resistance to death as part of growing older, Metchnikoff asked, like a good scientist, why. *Why should I revolt against what is the natural course of things? Other natural processes come upon me willingly: by the time I need sleep, I am sleepy, when I need food I am hungry and then after eating satisfied. Why do I not feel satisfied with life as my end grows nearer?* His conclusions were that we must in fact be meant to live much longer than we do and that something was somehow bringing about the premature aging and death of most of the humans on the planet.

To understand Metchnikoff's thinking, one must understand a little about the world in which he lived: even before anyone understood that the bowels were full of microbes, people believed the products of the bowels were unhealthy. In the eighteenth and nineteenth centuries, as cities grew densely populated before they developed effective sewage systems, people began to fear that even the foul odor from human waste could be unhealthy. Many claimed that diseases such as cholera, which spread in epidemic proportions in cities, were caused by the evil gases that emerged from the open sewers.

When proof emerged in the mid-nineteenth century that germs cause disease, it reinforced the idea that the contents of the bowel could be toxic. People began to speculate that all those microbes in the bowels could release toxins that could seep into the body. "Autointoxication" from these poisons was proposed as the cause of a whole horde of complaints, ranging from headache to violent criminal impulses.

It was in this atmosphere that Metchnikoff, when he contemplated human aging, began to suspect people were poisoned from within by their bowel microbes. Metchnikoff began to consider that animals like the horse, with long large intestines and therefore plenty of room for microbes, had shorter life spans than those with shorter intestines—such as the parrot. When we were more primitive animals, he reasoned, we needed plenty of room to hold our feces when we were busy running down prey, or being preyed on:

> *In order to void the contents of the intestines, mammals have to stand still and assume some particular position. Each act of this kind is a definite risk in the struggle for existence. A carnivorous mammal which, in the process of hunting its prey, had to stop from time to time, would be inferior to one which could pursue its course without pausing. So, also, a*

INFIRMERIE ET PHARMACIE.
LOBCAUX ASTRINGENS ET EMOLLIENS.

C'EST ICI.

French cartoon from the 1880s satirizing how obsessed people were with their bowel habits

herbivorous mammal, escaping from an enemy by flight, would have the better chance of surviving the less it was necessary for it to stand still.

In modern life, however, with no tigers breathing down our necks, we could follow the whims of nature more easily. Therefore, we no longer needed our colon, Metchnikoff concluded, and in fact, would be much better off without it, for the microbes it housed produced poisons that were gradually killing us as we absorbed them.

Having identified a probable culprit, Metchnikoff began

Advertisement from the 1970s that shows Metchnikoff's beliefs lived on after he died

to explore possible solutions. The most obvious was, if the colon was unnecessary, get rid of it. Metchnikoff pointed to examples of people who had survived after having their colons removed. In fact, there was a doctor in London who began to specialize in colon removal for patients so certain they were being poisoned by their colons that they were willing to go under the knife.

Nonetheless, the state of surgery being what it was at the turn of the twentieth century—lacking antibiotics, many patients died of infection—colon removal remained too dangerous to recommend. Despite his earnest strivings for immortality, Metchnikoff did not ask to have his cut out. Instead, he began to explore more benign methods of microbial reform. Taking his cue from the cheese makers, he began to wonder if a good microbe could be called on to overcome the bad. The microbe he thought might do it was *Lactobacillus bulgaricus*, or, as it came to be known, the Bulgarian bacillus. The Bulgarian bacillus, like other lactobacilli, sours milk and is used to make yogurt, particularly in parts of eastern Europe. In these regions, not only did people eat a lot of yogurt, but also a fair number lived to be at least a century old. For some observers, drawing a connection between yogurt eating and longevity was irresistible. (Even sixty years after Metchnikoff's death at least one well-known yogurt maker used the lined faces of old eastern Europeans eating yogurt in advertisements.)

Metchnikoff became convinced that the key to long life was to colonize the bowel with this Bulgarian bacillus in order to drive out the harmful organisms. In doing so, one could remove from the body the harmful toxins surely introduced by these organisms, and as a result not only live to age 120 or more but also be healthier in old age. Metchnikoff wrote, "It will be possible to modify old age [so that] instead of retaining its existing melancholy and repulsive character, it may become a healthy and endurable process."

The method Metchnikoff recommended for culturing the bowels was not to eat the yogurt, as that would introduce other microbes as well as the preferred Bulgarian one.

Rather, he suggested drinking sterilized milk or vegetable broth that had been injected with a pure culture of Bulgarian bacillus. Or else one could take dried culture in tablet form. Expecting doubters of his radical theories, Metchnikoff wrote, "A reader who has little knowledge of such matters may be surprised by my recommendation to absorb large quantities of microbes, as the general belief is that microbes are all harmful. This belief, however, is erroneous. There are many useful microbes, amongst which the lactic bacilli have an honourable place."

His gospel of yogurt became very popular, and Metchnikoff's works were published widely in French and translated into English as well. Doctors began to prescribe the bacillus to patients for a wide manner of ailments. In 1909 the Royal Society of Medicine had a session discussing the benefits of the bacillus.

Metchnikoff lived to age seventy-one. But as his life came to a close, nearly fifty years short of the age he hoped to attain, he was not disillusioned. He had always expected that it would take generations of "right living" before the human life span increased to its rightful length. And, in addition, he had lived an extremely full and intense life, perhaps more satisfying per year than the average life. After suffering a heart attack at sixty-eight, during his last three years he began to feel ready to die with the peace and satisfaction he had hoped for.

But soon after Metchnikoff's death, scientists found that the Bulgarian bacillus was not, in fact, a microbe that took up residence in the bowel. Thus, whatever its other merits, it could not drive out the supposedly poisonous bowel flora. Although the public still clamored for the Bulgarian bacillus, among the scientific community Metchnikoff's claims were considered unsupportable and fell into disrepute. Strangely enough, one hundred years later, the medical use of live cultures of lactobacilli is beginning to gain more and more respect. Although no one believes that we are being poisoned by our intestinal flora, or that getting rid of our large intestines would allow us to live to be 120, consuming live cultures of lactic acid bacilli has been found to treat and prevent some intestinal disorders.

These organisms can prevent the diarrhea that often occurs when you go to a new country, they can prevent takers of antibiotics who have killed off all their good gut microbes from being colonized with bad ones, and they can also treat different kinds of diarrhea caused by bad germs. Interestingly, the bugs you eat do not have to set up permanent residence in the gut to help fight off disease. It seems that if you take them every day, these good bugs can either prevent bad bugs from moving in or prevent them from spreading for just long enough to give the good microbes time to take over. Not only do they take up space in the intestine, but they also eat the nutrients the bad bugs need to survive. Moreover, their presence somehow turns our immune system on and makes it fight off the bad invaders more fiercely.

Metchnikoff was wrong on two points, however: Eating lactobacilli will not add fifty years to your life; and rather than poisoning us, the microbes in our guts are extremely important to our health. It is hard to blame Metchnikoff for his misunderstanding, though, for learning about the contributions of gut microbes has been very difficult. One of the biggest problems for researchers wishing to explore the inhabitants of our bowels has been that most of the microbes that grow in our colons will not grow in the labora-

MAKE LACTOBACILLI WORK FOR YOU

Interested in trying some of Metchnikoff's panacea? Even if you do not live to be 120, you may enjoy eating yogurt you made yourself. The key to yogurt making is getting the milk to the right temperature and keeping it there so the lactobacilli can reproduce happily. The best way to do this is to use a food thermometer.

• *Step 1:* Mix 1/3 cup instant nonfat dry milk into 1 quart pasteurized whole milk. Heat in a pan on the stove just to boiling and remove from the heat quickly, before the milk boils over.

Adding the dry milk makes a thicker yogurt. If you leave it out, you will get a tangy but thinner yogurt—similar to the yogurt eaten in much of Europe.

• *Step 2:* Let the milk cool to 120 degrees Fahrenheit. Time to use your thermometer!

• *Step 3:* Remove about 1/2 cup of the warm milk, place it in a small bowl or jar, add to it 2 heaping teaspoonfuls plain yogurt containing live active cultures. Mix well. Then pour this milk-and-yogurt mixture back into the rest of the warm milk and mix thoroughly.

tory. If one would take a fecal sample, for instance, and look for bacteria, one would see a wide variety of shapes and sizes. But if one took bits of that sample and placed them on a plate of bacteria food to grow more of them and see what each one would do, only about half of the wide variety of bugs would grow. No matter how well fed, warmed, and

---

Be sure to buy a commercial yogurt that says "live active cultures" on the container to use as the seed culture for making your yogurt. Buy plain yogurt; after your yogurt is finished, you can add any flavorings you like.

• *Step 4:* Now it is time to incubate. If you want to have small containers of yogurt, pour the milk mixture into small, clean glass jars with lids. (Jelly jars work nicely.) You can also keep it in one or more larger clean glass jars if you like. Place these jars in your incubator so they stay between 110 and 120 degrees Fahrenheit for 4 to 6 hours, or until thick. If 10 hours have passed and the mixture is still not thickened—time to start over.

There are various ways to incubate your yogurt. You can use a yogurt maker, which is basically a device that keeps several small containers warm for several hours while lactobacilli do all the work making the yogurt. Another idea is to get a cooler that your jars will fit into, fill it with 120-degree water so that it does not cover the lids of the jars, close the cooler lid, cover the cooler with thick towels or blankets, and allow the jars to incubate.

• *Step 5:* Store your finished product in the refrigerator. Enjoy!

A scanning electron micrograph of the lining of a rat intestine showing a group of bacteria at the letter B

otherwise coddled, the other half simply refuse to grow. Many can tolerate only the airless environment of the large intestine and die upon exposure to oxygen. The only way to study these creatures is to do so as they roam free in the formidable wilderness of the bowels.

The creatures that live in this wilderness are far too small to see with the naked eye. They each have their own habitat. Some prefer to exist midstream, mixed in with the continual flow of feces. Others live close to the bowel wall in tight little settled neighborhoods. A few are just visiting, having come in with the water or food of a new environment or via a change in the host's health. Yet others are more or less permanent residents, or at least their families are. Most bacteria reproduce by dividing, and any one single bacterium will exist for an average of twenty minutes before it splits into two—but at that rate, one bacterium can produce a billion progeny overnight. From our perspective, the diversity and complexity of the resulting community obscure the lifestyle and contributions, indeed the identity, of its individual members. How can we know how each individual species contributes to or detracts from its host's health? The solution would be to raise a creature without any microbes living in it at all. Then we could compare the microbe-free animal to the microbe-filled animal and see what was different.

Tore Midtvedt, a Norwegian researcher who has spent his career working on germ-free animals, still remembers the first time he laid eyes on a germ-free creature in the early 1960s. It was a rat, he recalls, and he was quite "impressed by this animal." Here was a creature who lived without the benefit of any microbes, a unique form of life. But what an effort was necessary to keep this creature alive! The stainless-steel box in which he lived, his food, and his water had to be heated under high pressure in order to kill any microbe life that might be lurking within. The very air he breathed had to be sterilized and filtered. His handlers reached into his cage through gloves securely attached to the box wall so as not to contaminate him through their touch or their breath. The gloves, the weakest link in the whole apparatus, were inspected regularly for breaks and frequently changed by an ingenious process of fitting a new sterile replacement glove over the old glove from the inside of the box and only then removing the old glove. The box could not be open to the outside for even an instant without risking infection.

Some German researchers were the first to attempt to raise a germ-free animal. Perhaps provoked by Pasteur's assertion that microbes were necessary for life, they delivered some guinea pigs by cesarean section to prevent them from being infected during birth and raised them germ-free for a short time. This experiment proved that life could continue—at least for a very short period—without microbes. It was nearly fifty years before this research was taken up again, this time with enough tools and expertise to prevent the infection of these creatures for their entire lifetime. Labs in the United States, Japan, and Sweden led the way in exploring what life was like without microbes. The initial animals were delivered by cesarean section in sterile operating rooms and then quickly whisked into their sterile living quarters. It was an incredible amount of work, Tore Midtvedt recalls, to be the foster mother for these rats. The scientists had to feed them sterile rat formula around the clock. Once a lab had raised a male and a female rat to adulthood germ-free, things became much simpler, as the couple could conceive germ-free offspring and deliver their progeny in their germ-free homes. The babies could be born naturally, for their mother's body housed no microbes that could infect them, and they could nurse from the mother, sparing the scientists long nights of feeding. Tore

Midtvedt's lab now features the hundredth generation of germ-free rats so raised.

The differences between these animals and those raised out in the germy world were dramatic illustrations of exactly how we rely on microbes. Very quickly it became clear that the creatures living within us make a difference. In the first place, the animals raised in the sterile environment grew to be somewhat bigger than those raised out in the germy world and lived about twice as long. (Metchnikoff would be glad to know this.) However, only if they were kept germ-free did they do so. If brought outside their bubble, they rapidly succumbed to infection. In fact, it was found that incredibly small numbers of germs completely overwhelmed them. Clearly, not only did the microbes in most creatures' guts make it harder for them to be infected with bad germs, but they had also trained their immune systems to fight off infection.

Another surprising thing was that although these germ-free animals could grow bigger than ordinary animals, they needed a lot more food to do so. Germ-free animals needed about 30 percent more calories in their diets simply to survive. Somehow, those microbes in our gut were helping us get more out of our food.

And germ-free creatures needed to be given all of their vitamin K. This vitamin, which we use to create a chemical that helps our blood clot, has since been found to be created by microbes that live in our guts. If we lose our gut flora—by having our colons removed or taking lots of antibiotics for a long time—we may also need to take vitamin K pills.

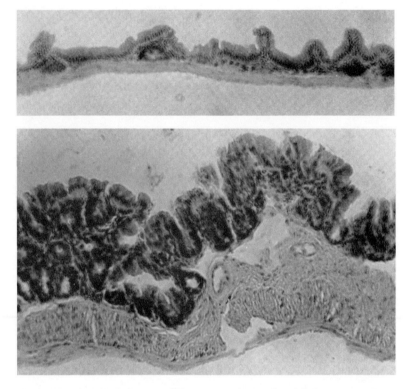

The intestinal wall of a mouse that was raised germ-free (top) and that of a mouse raised normally (bottom), showing the failure of the germ-free mouse's intestine to develop properly

Without the extra vitamin K, we would develop large bruises from the slightest bumps because our blood would not be able to clot properly.

And, strangely, the gut itself of the germ-free animals was different. One portion ballooned out, sometimes growing so big it got in the way of other internal organs. The gut walls did not contract correctly either. Somehow, the bugs in our gut help our gut become the right shape and size, and develop the right squeeze.

These results were the first proof of the contribution of microbes to our lives. But they were merely a superficial sketch of the whole picture. We still had no idea even what most of the microbes in the gut were. And we had no idea how profoundly they interacted with our digestive system. To understand that would take the development of a whole new set of tools that allowed scientists to examine an organism's blueprint for living. This blueprint is written in the chemicals RNA and DNA that make up the organism's genes.

It is only in the past fifty years that we have come to understand the significance of RNA and DNA. But in that time we have learned how to read the instructions encoded in the chemicals, so that now even bits of organisms can give us a clue to not only who they are but also what they do. Huge libraries listing genes can be accessed on the Internet. Let's say you have found some genetic material and you want to know what organism it came from. You can enter the sequence of the gene, or its genetic code, into a database and see if it matches anything anyone else has found and identified. But even beyond that, these databases also have information about what different stretches of code are known to do. So by comparing your mystery sequence with another sequence, you can get an idea about what an organism can and cannot do. The use of these tools throws a spotlight on the hard-to-explore depths of the bowel. Scientists have discovered more than five hundred species that live in our bowels, and a number of these species know some amazing tricks.

Certainly a spot in the human intestine is a choice place for a microbe—warm, dark, lots of food. This gives the microbes that live there plenty of incentive to stay and to keep invaders out. It has been observed that the types of microbes who move in first tend to be the types found in a person's gut throughout his or her life. Little by little, we are learning how these pioneers stake their claim.

The first settlers begin by interacting with the cells that line the gut and signaling these cells to create comfortable spots for them to attach to. The microbes also have ways to let the host gut cells know if they need a particular nutrient, and just how much of it they need. The cells that produce this nutrient for them will make just that amount, no more. That way there are no leftovers lying around for other newcomer microbes to eat.

Researchers working in Tore Midtvedt's lab were able to discover how deftly the microbes could manipulate our digestive system by cleverly using genetic tools. They found that the germ-free rats did not produce a certain ingredient in the mucousy slime normally protecting the walls of the intestines. Then they learned that one particular microbe—a bacterium that is a prominent member of normal gut flora of a genus known as *Bacteroides*—especially likes to dine on that mucous ingredient. Another lab had, coincidentally, found the gene for the enzyme that this type of *Bacteroides* used to digest the missing mucous ingredient and had created a mutant strain that lacked the gene and therefore could not use this particular food. Tore Midtvedt's lab workers decided to see what would happen if they took

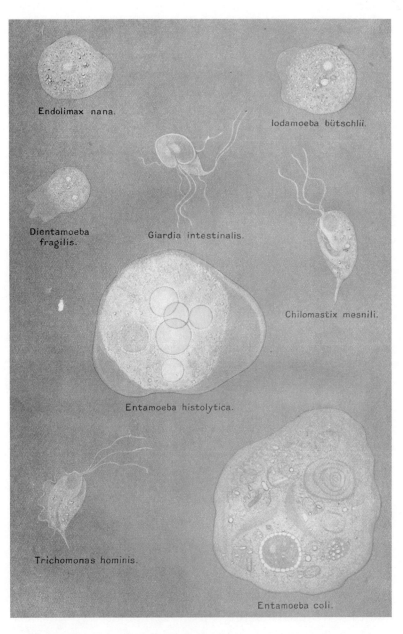

Endolimax nana.

Iodamoeba bütschlii.

Dientamoeba fragilis.

Giardia intestinalis.

Chilomastix mesnili.

Entamoeba histolytica.

Trichomonas hominis.

Entamoeba coli.

Depictions of common protozoa—single-celled, complex microorganisms— that live in the gut and can sometimes cause disease. These are about two thousand times life size

some germ-free rats and infected them with normal bacteria, and infected others with the mutant strain. The results were clear and dramatic: the intestines of the rats that now housed bacteroides began to produce the mucousy stuff. As if the bacteroides had turned on a tap to get a drink, the rat's intestines started to provide the microbe with the food it desired. However, in the intestines of the rats with the mutant bacteroides—the strain that did not eat this mucousy stuff—nothing new was produced. The bacteria had no need for this particular food and made no such demands, and the rat intestine therefore had no need to oblige.

This is a remarkable story of the type of interaction going on right now inside your gut between micro-organisms and you. We are just now developing the ability to listen in on this conversation. Who knows what else we will discover about how these microbes influence our lives?

One might imagine that with microbes in our guts eating all the time, we would need to eat more to feed them as well as ourselves. But the experiments with germ-free animals suggested just the opposite. Further exploration was certainly necessary. And this is what it revealed: instead of taking food from us, the microbes actually make indigestible bits of food digestible. Although we can digest a wide array of things, we don't do so well on the tough, complex material making up the cell walls of plants. Microbes, however, are good at breaking this down, and when they do, they extract what they need to grow, transforming what is left into something we can digest. This is a great arrangement for us: we don't have to develop the complex system necessary to do this digesting, but we still get the benefits. Not only that, but it gives us great flexibility. Let's say we travel and change our diet, incorporating a new type of plant product. All we have to do to be able to digest this new food is to grow a good crop of microbes that can. This is much easier than spending several hundred or several thousand years evolving gut cells with new digestive capacity.

In fact, recent studies suggest we depend on the microbes in our guts not only for the things that they can digest for us but even to be able to digest things well ourselves. By examining the genes of microbes in relation to the cells of our guts, scientists found that microbes "turn on" genes in those cells, enabling them to better digest many foods. Without the microbes, these genes exist but do not function. To be complete, we need the microbes!

Very recently gut microbes have been found to excrete their own antibiotics. They produce drugs that they can tolerate but that kill newcomers intent on moving in. This arrangement is good for the microbes and good for us. The microbes monopolize our gut as a habitat, and they also keep out invaders that might make us sick.

Having certain microbes inside us from such an early age appears to have another surprising benefit: these microbes train our immune system. A competent immune system is like a good watchdog—immune cells fight off invaders, but they also know not to bite family and friends. From the time we are infants, the microbes in our guts help teach our immune cells the difference; that is, they help them tell when and what to attack. Immune cells that attack indiscriminately can cause allergies and destroy healthy tissue. Although how our gut microbes train the immune system is complex and only partly understood, some researchers are becoming convinced that the rise in asthma and allergies seen in the wealthier countries of the world may be caused by the modern world being so clean that it keeps us away from the microbes we need to stay healthy.

Microbes have been on the planet since long before humans. All animals came to be in a world that was full of microbes. Since we have always lived with them, we have become interdependent with these tiny creatures. But, although our interdependence with microbes goes back to our very beginning, our understanding of this interdependence is so young, and such cutting-edge science, that discoveries are made every week.

Exploring these microbes is truly a new frontier—strangely, a frontier found inside of us. Some of what we can learn from these explorations is about our past: we can see in our interdependence the history of our many years of living with these microbes. And some of what we are learning will show us the future: from microbiology we discover new things about both microbes and our own bodies, how to improve our immune system, and new ways to treat everything from earaches to traveler's diarrhea. Certainly we are gaining a new appreciation for these creatures to whom we owe our lives.

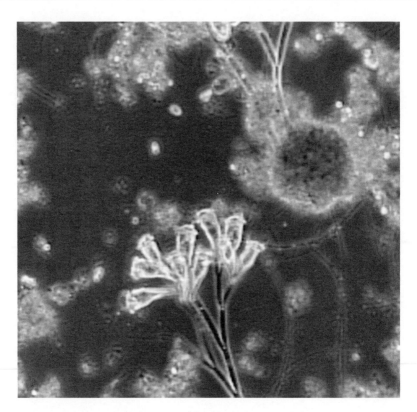

Epistylis rotans, stalked ciliate in activated sludge

Rot Away

If I should die before I wake,
All my bones and sinew take;
Put me in the compost pile,
And decompose me for a while.

Worms, water, rain will have their way,
Returning me to common clay!
All that I am will feed the trees,
And little fishes in the seas.

When radishes and corn you munch—
You might be having me for lunch!
And then excrete me with a grin—
Chortling, "There goes Lee again!!"
—"IN DEAD ERNEST" BY LEE HAYS,
A MEMBER OF THE FOLK GROUP THE WEAVERS

There are perhaps no greater favors microbes do for us than eating our poop when we live and eating us when we die. It is horrific to consider what would happen if microbes did not: an estimated 110 billion people have lived on Earth to this day. If the bodies of those people did not decompose, the entire land surface of the planet would be three deep in bodies. And that would be just the human bodies: as fascinating as it would be to see a real, intact, but dead tyrannosaur, the bodies of every tyrannosaur, woolly mammoth, elephant, giraffe, and every other animal that ever lived would make it difficult for us to move around. Of course, this is not to mention the trees and other plants, and not to mention the poop. A human produces nearly two hundred pounds of poop per year. One horse produces twelve tons on its high-cellulose diet. I need not go on: not only is it quickly clear that without some help we would soon be swamped by exactly those things we would rather not consider, but this scenario is completely impossible. Without the work of microbes eating dead bodies, dead plants, and poop, living things would run out of parts from which to make new life. Life on our planet would grind to a halt. By eating not only our waste but eventually our very selves, microbes both clean up a lot of mess and liberate the little bits of us so that new life can be made from them. That is the real heart of decomposition: it is necessary to take things apart in order to put them together again.

The fact that we owe it all to the magnificent appetites of microbes is abundantly clear on a visit to the wastewater treatment center that serves the part of Seattle where I live. Between the thick gunk that flows in, coming from toilets and drains throughout the city, and the water and fertilizer that come out just six to twelve hours later—headed for the

Bird's-eye view of a wastewater treatment plant

clear waters of Puget Sound and the wheat fields of eastern
Washington State, respectively—stands a host of hungry
microbes. And while the stuff that we flushed down the toilet makes its way through the treatment system, bubbling
in tanks as far as the eye can see, it is known by the operators of the plant as "food."

Jim Pitts, a senior process analyst at the South Treatment Plant near Seattle, considers his job one of the best in
the world. It is his duty to keep an uncountable number of
ravenous microbes happy and well fed. From his vantage
point in the laboratory of the treatment plant, he monitors

the workings of this vast microbial community, using sophisticated monitoring systems, computer simulations, and microscopes capable of videotaping the organisms' activity. With ninety million gallons of wastewater thundering toward his plant every day, he needs his microbes to be fighting ready.

For all of its fancy tanks, pipes, gauges, and alarms, the modern wastewater treatment plant is designed merely to do the work of a stream, but on a grand scale. Before there were wastewater treatment plants, the refuse from cities ended up in nearby rivers. In some civilizations, such as that of the Romans, waste flowed to rivers through well-designed pipes, and water for drinking came back in others, and the two were designed not to meet. In other places, such as the cities of Europe in the Middle Ages, which had no sewage systems, waste thrown into the streets was washed into rivers by the rain. The flowing river carried the waste away—out of sight, out of mind. And in the rivers, the microbes took care of things.

The waste was a virtual feast for all sorts of bacteria, protozoa, and fungi living in the streams. As they ate up the waste, they made available for other uses the elements nitrogen, sulfur, and phosphorus that were part of the waste. Living things need these elements to build their bodies. If, however, the amount of waste became too much, and as a result the microbes grew too quickly, they could overcrowd the stream and use up all the oxygen in the water. Not only would that suffocate plants and fish, but it would favor the growth of microbes that thrive without air. These creatures produce stinky gases when they eat. Soon such a stream would be black, slimy, stinky, and dead to all but those creatures who could live without oxygen.

In the nineteenth century, as cities grew quickly, their rivers fast became overwhelmed. By 1865 the river Thames, which flows through London, smelled so foul that Parliament canceled its meetings for the summer. And the stink was the least of it: the world was in the throes of successive cholera pandemics spread by drinking water contaminated by infected feces. Something had to be done.

A cartoonist's 1850 "microscopic" view of the sewage-infested river Thames

The solution was to build wastewater treatment plants that would collect waste, feed it to microbes, disinfect it, and release the elements. Key to this process would be always to give the microbes enough but not too much air.

In my house, all the drains—from the sink and the shower and the toilet—flow to the wastewater treatment plant, as do the storm drains on the street. (In some places the storm drains have a separate outflow.) As they roll along through miles of pipe on their way to the plant, they carry along some microbes—poop being 60 percent microbes, for

Primary settling tanks

instance—and they also pick up new ones. Microbes enter from the rain-washed streets, get picked up from the inside of the pipe, and come in from the soil through breaks in the pipe. The wastewater that reaches the treatment plant is rich in microbes very similar to those found in a stream. After bigger objects like sticks are combed out, the sewage moves slowly through large primary settling tanks in which the heavy, chunky stuff sinks to the bottom and the greasy stuff floats to the top. Both are skimmed off. Then the solids head to one part of the plant and the liquids to another.

This is when the microbes come to the fore. The liquids are sent to large "aeration basins." In these big tanks, air—or in some plants straight oxygen—is pumped into the fluid. Now all the microbes that thrive on lots of air, and find the "food" in the tanks appetizing, begin to eat and reproduce. They eat voraciously, so much so that by the time the wastewater flows out to clarifying basins to allow the remaining bacteria to settle, it has gone from a cloudy dark tan to a nearly clear fluid. The bits of human waste that clouded the water have been eaten by the microbes and turned into carbon dioxide and the stuff of their bodies. After the remaining microbes are killed by chlorine, and the chlorine is then removed, the water is ready to be released to Puget Sound. The microbes that settle to the bottom in the clarifying tanks are then pumped back into the aeration basins as a "starter" culture to get the whole process going again.

In many ways, the microbes run the plant. What an industry, with workers who labor for free. You don't even need to advertise to hire them: when the plant that my waste feeds first opened, the plant operators did not need to get a starter culture of microbes from another plant: they just started slowly—a little sewage at a time—and soon found that the right bugs had shown up for the job.

But the bugs do need supervision. If in their eager eating they outstrip their air supply, the plant, just like a stream, can go anaerobic—and then things get stinky fast. Jim Pitts and his team must monitor the unseen life in these tanks and, by watching its complex society evolve, judge the condition of the sewage.

Pitts takes a small bottle of liquid, a sample from a clarifying basin, shakes it to suspend the settled brown layer, and places a drop on a slide. Under the microscope, this lifeless-looking liquid reveals itself to be a swarming, intricate community. Across the field stretch the stick-like branches of the filamentous microbes, some of which are bacteria, some fungi. Darting across, too quick for the microscope to follow, comes a little oval protozoan, propelled by tiny hairlike cilia beating so fast they are a blur. Past the branches float clumps of bacteria, each tiny oval creature just one-hundredth the size of the protozoan. All are translucent and colorless in their watery world. Surveying the scene, after years of this work, Jim Pitts knows in one glance: "This is mature sludge."

Pitts's trained glance notices how much background cloudiness there is in the water and how many bacteria have formed discrete clumps. He evaluates what organisms there are in the water. Too many of the filaments, and they begin

Aeration basins

to act like parachutes, sticking to the clumps of bacteria and letting them drift toward the surface. Just the right amount, weighted down by a clump, can act "like a hairbrush" catching other clumps of bacteria in its "bristles" and bringing them along as it drifts toward the bottom.

All of these concerns are, of course, secondary to the organisms themselves. They are involved in their own dramas. While the bacteria are busy feeding on the bits of waste that float by, the protozoa are feeding on the bacteria. The darting protozoa set up a current with their whirling cilia that propel the hapless bacteria into their grasp.

The stalked ciliate, with its cuplike body standing on a long stem, looks just like a transparent tulip. A faint flutter of its cilia is the only movement revealing its predatory nature. In addition to sweeping bacteria inside, these creatures can retract their stem and spring out again, to prey not only on bacteria but also on other protozoa.

The walls of Jim Pitts's lab are full of portraits of the possible casts of characters and their nicknames. There is the shelled amoeba whose central hole earns it the name

NITROGEN CYCLE

One completely essential bit of recycling that we owe to microbes is the making of nitrogen available for plants and animals to use. Nitrogen is an element we need to build all the protein in our bodies and to make the chemicals that contain our genetic code. Luckily, there is plenty of nitrogen in the atmosphere. In fact, 80 percent of the air we breathe is nitrogen. The nitrogen in the air, however, is inert, which for an element is like being happily married: an inert element is so stable and content that it is not interested in reacting with any other molecules. That may be well and good for the nitrogen, but it means that we cannot coax it into making the parts of our body we need it to make. There are, however, bacteria capable of pulling this inert gas out of its stable state and into a usable form. These organisms, known as nitrogen fixers, live in the soil. Some work together with plants; others are free-living. Not only do bacteria pull nitrogen out of the atmosphere for our use but they break down organic matter and free up the nitrogen trapped in plants or animals for use by other organisms. Without them, we simply could not go on.

doughnut, and an oval-shaped relative, with horizontal zigzagging ridges, called the pineapple. There is also a roly-poly protozoon known as the water bear.

Pitts takes me out of the lab to see the plant in action. The place is a huge array of tanks, some round, some long, some open, some closed. Hardly a human is in sight: the bulk of the workers are invisible. The bubbling aeration basins are full of cloudy, frothing liquid that looks like weak coffee with milk, but smells quite different. I try to imagine each drop teeming with the interesting creatures I just saw under the microscope, but I am somewhat distracted by an irrational fear of falling in. Pitts is explaining to me the crises that can arise and require quick action. "Once we ended up with six feet of foam on the top of these tanks!" says Pitts with a twinkle in his eye. Standing on the narrow walkway between two tanks deep with bubbling brown fluid, I couldn't help but blurt out, "That sounds horrifying!" Pitts grinned. "It was pretty exciting."

Meanwhile, at the other end of the plant, the solids that sank out of the liquid river of sludge have been pumped into tanks with the very descriptive name of "digesters." In contrast to the open bubbling aerators, the digesters look like short fat columns. The solid water from our waste is a delight for anaerobic bacteria that thrive in their airless confines. Some break the waste down into acids; others, in turn, break the acids down into gases. This mixture of gases, known as biogas, is stinky as well as flammable. Beyond producing smelly farts, biogas can be a surgical hazard. If hot instruments are used to burn blood vessels closed in bowel surgery, sometimes the result can be explosive. When produced in a wastewater treatment plant, however, this gas can come to a useful end. In some plants, the biogas is captured in pipes and used not only to heat the plant but also to provide some of the plant's electricity.

I suppose, with eating being the business of the plant, it is not surprising that the sewage gets described as food. But I think the use of that word might also be sewage treatment "brown" humor. Jim Pitts showed me a sample of the sludge that enters the digester, a dark, thick green goop that in no way looked edible.

"It's the consistency of a thick milk shake," he said, tipping a liter sample bottle of the stuff to demonstrate. When he opened the bottle, the smell that rapidly filled the room made me hold my breath. After three to four weeks in the digester, he explained, reaching for another bottle, it would be "the consistency of heavy cream." As he began to unscrew this lid, I took one last deep breath, but he shook his head. "It's just musty smelling." And it was true. Still a swampy dark green, this stuff merely smelled like an old tent. In the treatment process the "heavy cream" is "dewatered," either in centrifuges or on long screens, until the final product is produced. Pitts gestured toward a pan spread with dark crumbly material that looked like nothing so much as spongy, very dark brownies. Pitts lifted some out with a spoon. "Cake!" he said with a smile.

This cake may not be good food for us, but for growing plants it proves to be a bonanza. Known as biosolids, the

Jim Pitts, with a sample of "cake"

microbes in this cake have concentrated the nutrients from the waste in forms that plants can use. In Seattle, the treatment plants sell it to farmers for about a dollar a ton. Huge double-trailer trucks carry biosolids over the mountain pass to the wheat and hop fields of the dry eastern part of the state. There this spongy material soaks up and holds rain, anchors the soil against marauding high winds, and offers the farmers' crops a wealth of nutrients. (If the biosolids are heated to kill any remaining disease-causing organisms, they can even be used in home gardens.)

It is remarkable to note how the poop that results from eating a sandwich can become biosolids to feed wheat that will be ground into flour that will be made into more bread that will, of course, make sandwiches! Through decomposi-

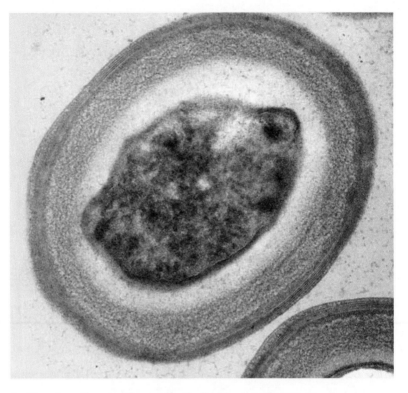

Bacillus stearothermophilus, **a microbe that loves to live in your nice warm compost pile**

tion, microbes complete the cycle, allowing life to be built from what was dead. And it is not just poop that they are decomposing. Let us not forget the scraps of our lunch that we have thrown onto our compost heap. Composting, a practice becoming popular not just with home gardeners but also with cities, is the transformation of yard or food waste into rich soil by, you guessed it, microbes.

Many readers are no doubt familiar with composting. Some add worms to their compost bins to aid in decomposition. Although worms and other insects—like millipedes, sow bugs, snails, and slugs—decompose compost, in each teaspoon of good compost there are billions of unseen contributors as well. Composting organisms work in sequence like those that team up to make cheese or ferment cacao. In the compost pile, their shifts are largely dictated by how hot it gets. Microbes work so hard that they can get a compost pile steaming hot. Although fungi are important in composting, as they can break down things other microbes cannot, the most numerous participants are the bacteria. Bacteria comfortable at room temperature—known as mesophiles—set to work, immediately degrading the easy-to-eat compounds in the bin. As they work, they heat things up, raising temperatures to well over 100 degrees Fahrenheit. Once it gets past about 104, though, these bugs start feeling a little too hot to keep going and so they slow down. That is when the heat-loving bacteria, the thermophiles, take over. The thermophiles break down the more complex, hard-to-digest bits of compost, heating things up still further in the process. If the compost pile is well insulated, temperatures can reach as high as 131 degrees. This heat can kill disease-causing germs, but it is not too much for the thermophiles! If left alone, and well fed, these organisms can outdo themselves, though. When they crank it up to 149 degrees, even they will start to falter, the mesophiles will die, and the compost will stop decomposing.

Key to a sweet-smelling compost pile is letting the bugs breathe. Just as was true in the stream and in wastewater treatment, too little air brings on the anaerobes and with them come stinky gases. The larger organisms help get air to the microbes; the trails left by worms' bodies are like a series of pipes delivering air throughout the pile. Mixing in bulky materials like straw can also create air pockets.

Microbes eat our poop, and microbes eat our garbage; in fact, it appears that if nature makes a substance, a microbe will eat it. With microbes swarming throughout the earth by the billion, all trying to get something to eat, those that are able to eat things other microbes leave untouched are more likely to come back from the microbe buffet with a full plate. As a result, microbes have evolved a wide variety of appetites. Substances that a microbe will break down are known as biodegradable. Some of these things we would rather they didn't eat. For instance, the wood of our house, the iron pipes through which our water runs, even the stone of buildings themselves have been degraded with the help of microbes. The Buddhist temple Angkor Wat in northwestern Cambodia is a sad example. The stone of the temple soaks up sulfide from the soil, and certain bacteria convert the sulfide to sulfuric acid, which degrades the ancient and beautiful temple.

Some man-made substances, however, are another story. Man-made chemicals that have been created just in this past century give evolution no chance to catch up. Walking along even the most remote beach, one comes across hunks of old coolers made of Styrofoam, one of the substances humans have created that microbes cannot relieve us of. (If your lunch came on a Styrofoam plate, microbes can't help you dispose of it.)

But although microbes cannot take care of all the

garbage we make, we are learning how to use them to clean up more and more of our messes, some much worse even than poop. On the night of March 24, 1989, the tanker *Exxon Valdez* struck Bligh Reef off the coast of Alaska, broke open, and poured about 11 million gallons of oil into the cold waters of Prince William Sound. As a result, some 350 miles of shoreline were contaminated—a distance greater than that from Boston to Philadelphia. An oil spill is catastrophic for sea life. It coats and smothers plants and seashore creatures. Oil slicks down the feathers of birds and the fur of seals, depriving these animals of the pockets of insulating air they need to survive in their cold environments. Preening birds poison themselves by ingesting the oil, and oil-coated eggs fail to hatch.

Oil spills have generally been cleaned up as much as possible with vacuums and hot-water washing—a method that

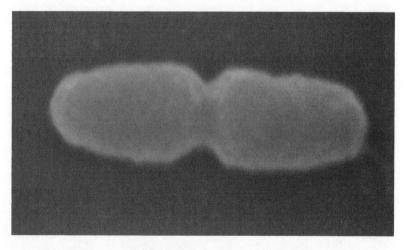

Azoarcus tolulyticus, a microbe that can eat toxins found in gasoline and is used to clean up spills above and below ground, and in the water

is so traumatic to some coastal creatures it may be just as bad as the oil. But this time another method was employed, one that had been observed and used a little but not really tried on a large scale. Microbes were encouraged to grow and eat up the oil. Bioremediation, as this method of cleaning up human spills is called, involves using microbes that eat toxins to convert them to harmless substances. Bioremediation can occur with no real human intervention: microbes that eat the toxin just step out of the soil and up to the buffet table, so to speak. But it may take them a very long time to clean up a big spill. Scientists have found that feeding the microbes some other things they need to grow,

Lake Berkeley

such as nitrogen and phosphorus, can speed things along. Since the *Exxon Valdez* spill, bioremediation has been used to clean up the worst kind of toxin spills all over the country. Today, at fifty Environmental Protection Agency Superfund sites—notorious industrial messes deemed priorities for cleanup—microbes are doing the work.

Scientists, meanwhile, are avidly searching for bacteria that can clean up more of our messes. Near Butte, Montana, lies a flooded open-pit mine called Lake Berkeley. The lake is a lake only in the sense that it is an inland body of water. This 850-foot-deep, 700-acre body of water in no way supports the fish, plants, and waterfowl we usually associate

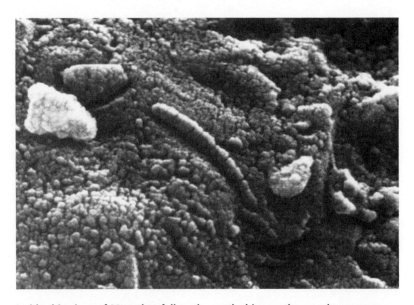

Inside this piece of Mars that fell to the earth thirteen thousand years ago scientists have found what some believe to be fossil microbes that may have lived on Mars some four or five billion years ago. By studying the microbes that live on Earth in extreme environments, scientists hope to understand better what forms of life might inhabit seemingly inhospitable places on other planets

with a lake. In fact, an oft-repeated story recalls how more than three hundred snow geese landed there one evening on their journey south in November 1995. In the morning every last bird was dead. The water is horribly acidic—comparable to lemon juice—and richly laced with metals such as copper, cadmium, and arsenic. Sulfide in the rock (exposed by mining to air and water) has been transformed into sulfuric acid.

Initially, scientists thought that no organisms could survive in the waters of Lake Berkeley, but to their amazement they discovered that some do. Microbes of many types, bacteria, algae, fungi, and protozoa somehow continue to exist, and some even thrive. To survive under conditions that are usually deadly, these organisms must be unique. There are some microbes that eat metals and others that temper acidic environments; scientists look upon them as possible sources of new life for Lake Berkeley. Their odd appetites could possibly transform the pit from a death pool to a clean lake—a place where a snow goose could safely float.

Bioprospectors are exploring more and more extreme environments in search of microbes that are happy there. They look in hot springs, in the driest deserts, in salt flats, under Antarctic ice—and they find microbes every time. These "extremophiles," with their odd ways, may be able to help us not only control our messes but also broaden our understanding of life. Some think that extremophiles might give us some insight into the forms of life that might exist on some hot, or cold, or acidic planet far off in space. In fact, the National Aeronautics and Space Administration (NASA) has dedicated its Astrobiology Institute to this task.

When I think of the microbes that are thriving in the acid waters of Lake Berkeley, I begin to feel as if microbes are small in size alone. Although we have not been blessed with eyesight that can naturally appreciate them, clearly the scale of microbes is vast in every other way. Microbes can live at temperatures twice as high as we can endure, and also survive twice the cold. They populate the full range of the earth, from below the ocean floor—a place we cannot endure—to high in the atmosphere where the air is so thin we would perish. And they even live in extremely salty, acidic, and dry-as-a-bone places where we would not stand a chance. In fact, their ability to survive outruns our puny perceptions of the limits of life. Their numbers are so overwhelming that the microbes in each handful of soil outnumber the entire human population on Earth.

Microbes were around for billions of years before humans and will likely continue to thrive long after we pass away. All of this is, in fact, some great comfort, as we could certainly not survive without them. They are the recyclers of the planet, invisibly keeping life going, and they are silent partners in our bodies, even collaborating with our genes. I, for one, would feel forever indebted to microbes for the creation of chocolate alone.

Now, reader, every bite of cheese, every bit of bread, and indeed every flush of the toilet can have new meaning for you. Your eyes have been refocused and you can look beyond the scale at which we live, knowing you are surrounded by communities of microbes hard at work. Some very few of them are capable of sickening us, it is true, but far more are doing the most essential work on the planet, invisibly.

Glossary

Notes and Bibliography

Illustration Credits

Index

Glossary

Anti-microbial A drug that kills or inhibits the growth of a microorganism.

Bacillus (Plural: *bacilli*) A rod-shaped bacterium.

Bacterium (Plural: *bacteria*) A simple, single-celled microorganism important in medicine because some bacteria cause disease.

Budding To reproduce asexually by means of growing out of a "parent."

Decomposition The process of decay.

Flora Microbes that live on or in a host organism.

Fungus (Plural: *fungi*) Any of a group of plantlike organisms that either are parasites or live on decaying matter.

Genes The units of the genetic code, each of which codes for a particular protein.

Genetic Having to do with the genes.

Germ A microorganism, particularly one that causes disease.

Hyphae Thready branches of a fungus.

Immune response The interaction of the immune system with foreign proteins.

Lactobacillus (Plural: *lactobacilli*) A rod-shaped bacterium that produces lactic acid.

Microbe A form of life too small to see with the naked eye. (A microorganism.)

Microbiology The study of microscopic forms of life.

Microorganism A form of life too small to see with the naked eye. (A microbe.)

Mold A microscopic plant that grows especially on damp or decaying organic material or on living organisms and that reproduces by means of spores.

Protozoon (Plural: *protozoa*) Single-celled organism; some protozoa are parasites.

Spores Very tiny, long-lasting seeds produced by some plants and microorganisms.

Virus A type of submicroscopic germ that cannot reproduce without infecting a living cell.

Yeast A sugar-eating single-celled fungus that reproduces by means of budding.

Notes and Bibliography

In researching this book I read countless articles and books, consulted many Internet resources, and talked to quite a few helpful and informative people. Included below are the books and conversations that contributed most significantly to the book, as well as source notes for direct quotes.

Introduction

Notes

3   "For creatures your size": W. H. Auden, *Collected Poems*, Edward Mendelson, ed. (New York: Vintage, 1991), 838.

5   "If we summarize": Rahn, *Microbes of Merit*, 145.

7   "I saw therein": Dobell, *Antony van Leeuwenhoek and His "Little Animals,"* 132–33.

10   "I did see a very great" . . . "I did see those little animals": Ibid., 175.

10   "For my own part": Ibid., 201.

12   "I then most always saw": Ibid., 239.

12   "an unbelievably great": Ibid., 241–42.

14   "Globules of Blood": Ibid., 319.

Bibliography

Digital Learning Center for Microbial Ecology, Michigan State University. www.commtechlab.msu.edu/sites/dlc-me/index.html.

Dixon, Bernard. *Power Unseen: How Microbes Rule the World.* New York: Oxford University Press, 1996.

Dobell, Clifford. *Antony van Leeuwenhoek and His "Little Animals": Being Some Account of the Father of Protozoology and Bacteriology and His Multifarious Discoveries in These Disciplines, Collected, Translated, and Edited from His Printed Works, Unpublished Manuscripts, and Contemporary Records.* New York: Russell and Russell, 1958.

Levy, Stuart B. "Antibacterial Household Products: Cause for Concern." *Emerging Infectious Diseases*, vol. 7, no. 3 (June 2001), 512–15.

———. "The Challenge of Antibiotic Resistance." *Scientific American*, vol. 278, no. 3 (March 1998), 46–53.

Postgate, John. *Microbes and Man.* New York: Penguin, 1986.

Rahn, Otto. *Microbes of Merit.* Lancaster, Pa.: Jacques Cattell Press, 1945.

Van Denmark, Paul J., and Barry Batzing. *The Microbes: An Introduction to Their Nature and Importance.* San Francisco: Benjamin-Cummings, 1987.

Microbes at the Table

Notes

19 "Cheese—milk's leap": Clifton Fadiman, *Any Number Can Play* (Cleveland: World, 1957), 105.

Bibliography

Beresford, Tom, et al. "Recent Advances in Cheese Microbiology." *International Dairy Journal*, vol. 11, no. 4 (July 2001), 259–74.

Bilger, Burkhard. "Raw Faith." *The New Yorker,* vol. 78, no. 24 (August 19 and 26, 2002), 150–54.

Brothwell, Don, and Patricia Brothwell. *Food in Antiquity*. Baltimore: Johns Hopkins, 1969.

Davidson, Alan. *The Penguin Companion to Food*. New York: Penguin, 2002.

Grace, Julia, and Susan Grace. Interview with author at Moonstruck Organic Cheese, Inc., Salt Spring Island, British Columbia, Canada, March 17, 2003.

Jenkins, Steve. *Cheese Primer*. New York: Workman, 1996.

Marcellino, Noella, et al. "Diversity of *Geotrichum candidum* Strains Isolated from Traditional Cheesemaking Fabrications in France." *Applied and Environmental Microbiology*, vol. 67 (October 2001), 4752–59.

———. "Scanning Electron and Light Microscopic Study of Microbial Succession on Bethlehem St. Nectaire Cheese." *Applied and Environmental Microbiology*, vol. 58 (November 1992), 3448–54.

McCalman, Max, and David Gibbons. *Cheese Plate*. New York: Clarkson Potter, 2002.

Roquefort Société. www.roquefort-societe.com.

Shephard, Sue. *Pickled, Potted and Canned: How the Art and Science of Food Preserving Changed the World*. New York: Simon & Schuster, 2001.

Tannahill, Reay. *Food in History*. New York: Three Rivers Press, 1989.

Thom, Charles. *The Book of Cheese*. New York: Macmillan, 1918.

Werlin, Laura. *The New American Cheese*. New York: Stewart, Tabori and Chang, 2000.

Our Daily Bread

Notes

45   "There's something alive": Ed Wood. "Sourdoughs: From Antiquity, to Today and Tomorrow." 1999. http://food .oregonstate.edu/ref/culture/wood.html.

46   "in the shadow" . . . "real bread": www.sourdo.com/ culture.htm.

52   "What fermentation" . . . "Louis . . . is up to his neck": Debré, *Louis Pasteur*, 87.

55   "The Vienna Bakery": Wright, *125 Years and Still Rising*.

Bibliography

Allman, Ruth. *Alaska Sourdough*. Anchorage: Alaska Northwest Publishing, 1976.

Debré, Patrice. *Louis Pasteur*. Elborg Forster, trans. Baltimore: Johns Hopkins University Press, 1998.

Gobbetti, M. "The Sourdough Microflora: Interactions of Lactic Acid Bacteria and Yeasts." *Trends in Food Science and Technology*, vol. 9, no. 7 (July 1998), 267–74.

Jacob, H. E. *Six Thousand Years of Bread: Its Holy and Unholy History*. New York: Lyons Press, 1944.

Kline, Leo, and T. F. Sugihara. "Microorganisms of the San Francisco Sour Dough Bread Process." *Applied Microbiology*, vol. 21, no. 3 (March 1971), 459–65.

Lavermicocca, Paola, et al. "Purification and Characterization of Novel Antifungal Compounds from the Sourdough *Lactobacillus plantarum* Strain 21B." *Applied and Environmental Microbiology*, vol. 66, no. 9 (September 2000), 4084–90.

Pascualy, George. Interview with author at the Essential Bakery, Seattle, Washington, March 18, 2003.

Sheppard, Ronald, and Edward Newton. *The Story of Bread*. London: Routledge and Kegan Paul, 1957.

Sourdoughs International. www.sourdo.com.

Wing, Daniel, and Alan Scott. *The Bread Builders: Hearth Loaves and Masonry Ovens*. White River Junction, Vt.: Chelsea Green Publishing, 1999.

Wood, Ed. Personal communication with author, March 19, 2003.

———. *Classic Sourdoughs: A Home Baker's Handbook*. Berkeley: Ten Speed Press, 2001.

———. *World Sourdoughs from Antiquity*. Berkeley: Ten Speed Press, 1996.

Wright, Steven L. *125 Years and Still Rising: The History of the Fleischmann's Yeast Company 1868–1993*. San Francisco: Fleischmann's Yeast Co., 1992.

Food of the Gods

Notes

71   "The chief value": Acosta, *Natural and Moral History of the Indies*, 210.

72   "These the Indians": Colón, *The Life of the Admiral Christopher Columbus*, 232.

75   "cups of fine gold": Coe, *The True History of Chocolate*, 94.

77   "[Cacao seems] more suited": Benzoni, *History of the New World*, 150.

Bibliography

Acosta, José de. *Natural and Moral History of the Indies*. Jane E. Mangan, ed., and Frances M. Lopez-Morillas, trans. Durham, N.C.: Duke University Press, 2002.

Battock, Mike and Sue Azam-Ali. *Fermented Fruits and Vegetables: A Global Perspective.* Rome: Food and Agriculture Organization of the United Nations Services Bulletin, no. 134, 1998.

Benzoni, Girolamo. *History of the New World.* Translated and edited by W. H. Smyth. London: Printed for the Hakluyt Society, 1857.

Coe, Sophie D., and Michael D. Coe. *The True History of Chocolate.* London: Thames and Hudson, 1996.

Colón, Ferdinand. *The Life of the Admiral Christopher Columbus by His Son Ferdinand.* Translated and annotated by Benjamin Keen. New Brunswick, N.J.: Rutgers University Press, 1959.

Fermented Grain Legumes, Seeds and Nuts: A Global Perspective. Rome: Food and Agriculture Organization of the United Nations Services Bulletin, no. 142, 2000.

Haard, Norman, et al. *Fermented Cereals: A Global Perspective.* Rome: Food and Agriculture Organization of the United Nations Services Bulletin, no. 138, 1999.

Hendrix, Steve. "Chocolate Takes Flight." National Wildlife Federation. www.nwf.org/internationalwildlife/1998/cacao.html.

Mollison, Bill. *The Permaculture Book of Ferment and Human Nutrition.* Tyalgum, Australia: Tagari Publications, 1993.

Office of International Affairs National Research Council. *Applications of Biotechnology to Traditional Fermented Foods.* Washington, D.C.: National Academy Press, 1992.

Ostovar, K., and P. G. Keeney. "Isolation and Characterization of Microorganisms Involved in the Fermentation of Trinidad's Cacao Beans." *Journal of Food Science,* vol. 38 (1973), pp. 611–17.

Presilla, Maricel. *The New Taste of Chocolate.* Berkeley: Ten Speed Press, 2001.

Microbes Are Us

Notes

97   "The human body": Hooper et al., "Host-Microbial Symbiosis," 336.

102   "In order to void": Metchnikoff, *Prolongation of Life*, 65.

105   "It will be possible": Metchnikoff, *Nature of Man*, 263.

106   "A reader who has little knowledge": Metchnikoff, *Prolongation of Life*, 181.

111   "impressed by this animal": Midtvedt, interview.

Bibliography

Coates, M. E. *The Germ-Free Animal in Research*. New York: Academic Press, 1968.

Falk, Per G., et al. "Creating and Maintaining the Gastrointestinal Ecosystem: What We Know and Need to Know from Gnotobiology." *Microbiology and Molecular Biology Reviews*, vol. 62, no. 4 (December 1998), 1157–70.

Gest, Howard. *The World of Microbes*. Madison, Wis.: Science Tech Publishers, 1987.

Guarner, Francisco, and Juan R. Malagelada. "Gut Flora in Health and Disease." *The Lancet*, vol. 361, no. 9356 (February 8, 2003), 512.

Hooper, Lora V., et al. "Host-Microbial Symbiosis in the Mammalian Intestine: Exploring an Internal Ecosystem." *BioEssays*, vol. 20, no. 4 (December 1998), 336–43.

———. "How Host-Microbial Interactions Shape the Nutrient Environment of the Mammalian Intestine." *Annual Review of Nutrition*, vol. 22 (July 2002), 283–307.

Metchnikoff, Elie. *The Nature of Man: Studies in Optimistic Philosophy*. New York: G. P. Putnam's Sons, 1910.

————. *The Prolongation of Life: Optimistic Studies.* New York: G. P. Putnam's Sons, 1908.

Metchnikoff, Olga. *Life of Elie Metchnikoff.* P. Chalmers Mitchell, ed. New York: Knickerbocker, 1908.

Midtvedt, Tore. Phone interview with author, May 20, 2003.

Postgate, John. *Microbes and Man.* New York: Penguin, 1986.

Rahn, Otto. *Microbes of Merit.* Lancaster, Pa.: Jacques Cattell Press, 1945.

Todar, Kenneth. "The Normal Bacterial Flora of Animals." University of Wisconsin, Department of Bacteriology. www.bact.wisc.edu/Bact330/lecturenf.

Van Denmark, Paul J., and Barry Batzing. *The Microbes: An Introduction to Their Nature and Importance.* San Francisco: Benjamin-Cummings, 1987.

Whorton, James C. *Inner Hygiene: Constipation and the Pursuit of Health in Modern Society.* New York: Oxford University Press, 2000.

Rot Away

Notes
130–34 "This is mature sludge" . . . "Cake!": Pitts, interview.

Bibliography
Cornell Composting. http://compost.css.cornell.edu/Composting_home page.html.

Dobb, Edwin. "New Life in a Death Trap." *Discover*, vol. 21, no. 12 (December 2000), 86–92.

Environmental Protection Agency Superfund. www.epa.gov/superfund/sites.

Environmental Protection Agency. "The History of Drinking Water Treatment," February 2000. www.epa.gov/safewater/sdwa/trends .html.

Gest, Howard. *The World of Microbes*. Madison, Wis.: Science Tech Publishers, 1987.

Hammond, Rick. Interview with author at West Point Treatment Plant, Seattle, Washington, May 29, 2003.

Matthews, Mark. "Could a Toxic Lake Yield Life-Saving Microbes?" *Washington Post*, March 8, 1999, A9.

Pitts, Jim. Interview with author at South Treatment Plant, Renton, Washington, June 2003.

Postgate, John. *Microbes and Man*. New York: Penguin, 1986.

Wisconsin Department of Natural Resources. "The Microbiology of Activated Sludge," April 2003. www.dnr.state.wi.us/org/water/wm/ ww/tech/biol.htm.

Illustration Credits

Index

Page references in italics indicate illustrations.